U0483736

符号中国 SIGNS OF CHINA

中国古桥

CHINESE ANCIENT BRIDGES

"符号中国"编写组 ◎ 编著

中央民族大学出版社
China Minzu University Press

图书在版编目(CIP)数据

中国古桥：汉文、英文 /"符号中国"编写组编著. —北京：
中央民族大学出版社，2024.8
（符号中国）
ISBN 978-7-5660-2283-7

Ⅰ.①中… Ⅱ.①符… Ⅲ.①桥—古建筑—介绍—中国—汉、英 Ⅳ.①K928.78

中国国家版本馆CIP数据核字（2024）第017053号

符号中国：中国古桥 CHINESE ANCIENT BRIDGES

编　　著	"符号中国"编写组
策划编辑	沙　平
责任编辑	李苏幸
英文指导	李瑞清
英文编辑	邱　械
美术编辑	曹　娜　郑亚超　洪　涛
出版发行	中央民族大学出版社
	北京市海淀区中关村南大街27号　　邮编：100081
	电话：（010）68472815（发行部）　传真：（010）68933757（发行部）
	（010）68932218（总编室）　　　　（010）68932447（办公室）
经 销 者	全国各地新华书店
印 刷 厂	北京兴星伟业印刷有限公司
开　　本	787 mm×1092 mm　1/16　印张：11.5
字　　数	165千字
版　　次	2024年8月第1版　2024年8月第1次印刷
书　　号	ISBN 978-7-5660-2283-7
定　　价	58.00元

版权所有　侵权必究

"符号中国"丛书编委会

唐兰东　巴哈提　杨国华　孟靖朝　赵秀琴

本册编写者

乔　虹

前言 Preface

在中华大地上，随处可见各式各样的古桥。在材质上，有木桥、竹桥、石桥、砖桥、铁桥；在建筑形式上，有梁桥、索桥、拱桥、浮桥等等。这些各种各样的桥梁作为古代工程技术发展的结晶，千百年来不仅沟通着交通要道，维系着经济贸易的命脉，同时也传承着中国深厚的传统文化，反映了古人的建筑技术和审美情趣。这些古桥以或雄伟、或轩朗、或柔美的身姿点缀着祖国的锦绣河山。

China has a rich variety of ancient bridges everywhere in its vast land. There are bridges built in different materials such as timber, bamboos, stones, bricks and irons, and in various architectural styles such as beam, suspension, arch and floating bridges. Representing the achievements of the ancient engineering technology, these bridges became transportation arteries, which helped to maintain the economic and trade lifelines in ancient China. They also inherited the profound traditions of Chinese culture and

本书讲述了中国古桥的诞生与发展、桥梁的建筑艺术，并且着重介绍了中国各地留存至今的历史名桥，其中包括这些桥的建造缘起、建筑形式、装饰特点和典故传说。希望读者通过了解中国古桥，对中国传统文化的内涵有进一步的认识。

demonstrated the technical mastery and aesthetic taste of the ancient Chinese. The beautiful landscape of China is dotted with these magnificent, splendid and elegant ancient bridges.

This book provides an account of the birth and development of Chinese ancient bridges and the architectural art of bridge building. Specifically, the book walks through each of the historically well-known bridges in China including the origin of its construction, architectural style, decoration characteristics and related legends. The intention is to help readers gain a deeper understanding of the connotation of Chinese traditional culture through ancient bridges in China.

目 录 Contents

🟥 桥的历史
History of Bridges 001

原始的桥
Primitive Bridges 002

历代造桥
Bridge Building in Different Dynasties............. 006

古桥的建筑材料
Ancient Bridge Building Materials 013

🟥 桥的艺术
Art of Bridges 017

桥梁的建筑形式
Bridge Structures 018

桥梁的装饰
Bridge Decorations 029

🟥 各地名桥
Famous Bridges... 035

金水桥
Golden Water Bridges *(Jinshui Qiao)*............... 038

断虹桥
Broken Rainbow Bridge *(Duanhong Qiao)* 041

金鳌玉蛛桥
Bridge of Golden Turtle and
Rainbow *(Jin'ao Yudong Qiao)* 043

堆云积翠桥
Bridge of Cloud Gathering and
Greens Overlapping *(Duiyun Jicui Qiao)* 045

1

十七孔桥
Seventeen-Arch Bridge (Shiqikong Qiao) 048

绣漪桥
Colorful Ripples Bridge (Xiuyi Qiao) 052

卢沟桥
Lugou Bridge 059

永通桥
Yongtong Bridge 064

赵州桥
Zhaozhou Bridge 068

桥楼殿
Bridge-Tower Hall (Qiaolou Dian) 071

七孔桥
Seven-Arch Bridge (Qikong Qiao) 073

小商桥
Xiaoshang Bridge 076

永安石桥
Yong'an Stone Bridge 078

鱼沼飞梁
Flying Bridge across the Fish
Pond (Yuzhao Feiliang) 080

放生桥
Fangsheng Bridge 084

云间第一桥
Yunjian No. 1 Bridge 087

金莲桥
Golden Lotus Bridge (Jinlian Qiao) 089

七瓮桥
Seven-Urn Bridge (Qiweng Qiao) 091

宝带桥
Precious Belt Bridge (Baodai Qiao)................. 094

枫桥
Maple Bridge (Feng Qiao) 096

灭渡桥
Miedu Bridge 099

吴门桥
Wumen Bridge 101

大虹桥
Big Rainbow Bridge (Dahong Qiao) 104

五亭桥
Five Pavilions Bridge (Wuting Qiao)................ 106

断桥
Broken Bridge (Duan Qiao) 111

拱宸桥
Gongchen Bridge... 114

八字桥
Bazi Bridge.. 116

熟溪桥
Shuxi Bridge 118

彩虹桥
Rainbow Bridge (Caihong Qiao)...................... 121

万年桥
Thousand-Year Bridge (Wannian Qiao)............ 123

三峡桥
Three Gorges Bridge 125

渌水桥
Lushui Bridge... 128

龙脑桥
Loong Head Bridge (Longnao Qiao)................ 130

3

安澜桥
Anlan Bridge 132

泸定桥
Luding Bridge 137

霁虹桥
Rainbow Bridge *(Jihong Qiao)* 140

双龙桥
Double-Loong Bridge *(Shuanglong Qiao)* 143

梓里桥
Hometown Bridge *(Zili Qiao)* 145

普修桥
Puxiu Bridge 148

祝圣桥
Zhusheng Bridge 150

洛阳桥
Luoyang Bridge 152

安平桥
Anping Bridge 156

江东桥
Jiangdong Bridge 158

东关桥
Dongguan Bridge 160

湘子桥
Xiangzi Bridge 162

程阳桥
Chengyang Bridge 165

仙桂桥
Xiangui Bridge 167

花桥
Flower Bridge *(Hua Qiao)* 169

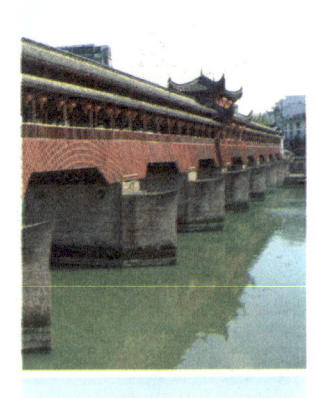

桥的历史
History of Bridges

　　中国是有着悠久历史和灿烂文化的文明古国，造桥的历史同样相当久远。几千年来，中国人在长河急流之间架起了一座座坚固而美观的桥梁，它们飞跨两岸，使天堑变为通途。

China is a country with a long history and a splendid culture of ancient civilizations. Bridge building in China witnessed an equally long history. Over the past several thousand years, the Chinese constructed enduring and beautiful bridges one after another across long and raging rivers making walkways possible over natural gorges.

> 原始的桥

自然界由于地壳运动或其他自然现象的影响，形成了不少天然的桥梁形式，比如河边的大树被风吹倒，恰巧横跨在河上，形成了天然的"梁桥"；两岸之间有藤萝悬跨，成为天然的"索桥"；两山中间的瀑布被石脊所阻，在流水的长期冲刷下，石脊的孔隙被磨成圆形，形成了天然的石拱桥……远古时代的人们从这些自然界的桥梁中得到启发，创造了最早的人造桥梁。

在陕西西安半坡村新石器时代的氏族聚落遗址（公元前4800—前4200）中，人们发现在部落周围挖有宽、深各5米左右的大围沟。据专家推测，这是为了防御野兽袭击和异族侵略，而氏族成员出入肯定有桥。不过由于材料和工艺的原因，

> Primitive Bridges

Nature created many bridge-like structures as a result of crustal movements or other natural phenomena. For example, a strong wind blew down a big riverside tree, which happened to fall across the river functioning as a natural beam bridge; vines growing from both sides of a river turned into a natural suspension bridge; a waterfall blocked by a cliff could make a small rock crevice eroded by water gradually into a natural arch across a gully. The ancient Chinese were inspired by these natural bridges and constructed the earliest man-made bridges.

In the Neolithic clan settlement ruins of Banpo Village near Xi'an, Shaanxi Province (4800 B.C.-4200 B.C.) archeologists discovered a moat of about 5m in depth and width surrounding the settlement. Experts believe that clan members must have used a bridge to enter or go out of

● 广西乐业布柳河天生桥（图片提供：全景正片）

广西乐业县境内的布柳河上，有一座由三座大山塌陷形成的天然石拱桥。桥拱对称，拱底平滑，当地人称为"仙人桥"。拱孔跨度177.14米，桥宽19.3米，桥身长280米，拱高87米，像一条巨龙横跨在河的两岸，可谓鬼斧神工。

Natural Arch on Buliu River, Leye County, Guangxi Zhuang Autonomous Region

Spanning the Buliu River in Leye County, Guangxi Zhuang Autonomous Region is a meander natural arch bridge cut through limestone karst by the river. The arch is symmetric and has a smooth bottom. The locals call it the "Fairy Bridge." The bridge is 19.3m wide and 280m long with a 177.14m span and an 87m high arch. It looks like a gigantic loong lying across the river as if it was the work of deities.

原始桥梁无法在漫长的岁月中保存下来。

　　从西周到春秋战国时期，是中国古代桥梁建筑的创始阶段。虽然当时人们已经学会了建造桥梁，但由于种种原因，在一般情况下还达不到遇水架桥的水平，尤其是西周时期，人们遇到较浅的河流，总是涉水而过。先秦时期第一部诗歌总

the settlement in order to fight against attacks from other tribes or wild animals. However it is impossible to preserve these original bridges over very long years due to the materials and techniques used to build them.

　　The beginning stage of the building history of Chinese ancient bridges is between the Western Zhou Dynasty (1046 B.C.-771 B.C.) and the Spring and

集《诗经》中就有很多关于涉水的诗句，比如《郑风·褰裳》中"子惠思我，褰裳涉溱"的意思是：你若思念我，就赶快蹚过溱河来找我。而对于较深的河流，人们就借助舟楫或者游泳渡过。在周代鲁国的故都（今山东曲阜）周围，人们发现了用于修建桥梁基台的石料和夯土层。

Autumn Period (770 B.C.-476 B.C.). Although at that time people learned to build bridges, generally they did not reached the level to erect a bridge over water due to various reasons. Especially in the Western Zhou Dynasty people always waded through shallow rivers. The first poetry collection *The Book of Songs* of the early Qin Dynasty has many verses about wading the river such as "if you miss me, wade the Qinhe River to come and see me". For deeper rivers, people usually crossed them by riding a boat or by swimming. In the capital of the ancient State of Lu (current Qufu City, Shandong Province) in the Zhou Dynasty, stones and rammed earth for building bridge foundations were discovered.

In the Spring and Autumn Period, there were mainly two types of bridges, beam bridges and floating bridges in addition to more primitive single-plank

● 四川广元古栈道（图片提供：FOTOE）
栈道桥起源于周代，在战国时期得到了很大发展。
Guanyuan Ancient Plank Road in Sichuan Province
Plank road bridges started in the Zhou Dynasty and developed quickly during the Warring States Period (475 B.C.-221 B.C.)

春秋时期的桥梁除了原始的独木桥和汀步桥外，主要有梁桥和浮桥两种形式。由于生产力水平落后，多数桥只能建在地势平坦、河身不宽、水流平缓的地段，形制也仅为木梁式的小桥。而在水面较宽、水流较急的河道上，则多采用浮桥。《诗经·大雅·大明》记载，周文王迎亲时，曾在渭河上"造舟为梁"，排列船只，跨船铺板，搭成浮桥。

and stone stepping bridges. Due to the backward productivity, most bridges were small timber-beam bridges built on flat areas across relatively narrow rivers with gentle water flow. Floating (pontoon) bridges were most used for wider rivers with more rapid water flow. *The Book of Songs* records that King Wen of the Zhou Dynasty had timber planks laid on top of the boats lined up in a river to make a floating bridge to welcome his bride.

多木梁结构的柱桥——栈道

栈道就是一种多木梁结构的柱桥。在无法通行的山崖峭壁上凿出孔，把木桩插进石孔中，固定结实，再在木桩上平铺木板，便成为可以通行的栈道了。有的栈道上层搭顶篷用来遮雨防晒，中层铺板用来行走，下层专做支撑用，使栈道更加坚实。战国时秦惠文王始建陕西褒城褒谷至郿县（今眉县）斜谷的褒斜栈道，长235千米。秦国伐蜀时又修了金牛道，被后世称为"南栈道"，长247.5千米。直至今日，在交通闭塞的山区，仍有类似的栈道供人畜通行。

Plank Road – The Bridge of Multi-Beam Structure

Plank roads along the cliffs are a type of beam bridges. They are built along steep cliffs by inserting and securing wooden beams into the rocks and then laying planks on top of them. To make it more secure and safer, some plank roads have three levels: the upper level is used as a cover against rain and sunshine; the middle level is the walking path; and the lower level supports the middle level. During the Warring States Period King Huiwen of the State Qin built the 235,000m long Baoxie Plank Path in today's Meixian County, Shaanxi Province. During the Qing Dynasty another plank road known as "Golden Cattle Path" or "South Plank Path" was built at a total length of 247,500m. Even today, plank roads are used as walking paths by travelers and their livestock in isolated and remote mountain areas.

> 历代造桥

秦汉时期是中国建筑史上一个重要的发展阶段，这一时期不仅出现了人造的建筑材料——砖，而且工匠们还创造出了以砖石结构为主的拱券结构，为后来拱桥的出现创造了条件。而战国时期铁器的出现，也提高了人们对石料的加工能力，从而使桥梁在木构梁桥的基础上，增添了石柱、石梁、石桥面

- "驭马过桥"画像石拓片（汉）

Stone Rubbings: *Riding a Horse Across the Bridge*, Han Dynasty (206 B.C. – 220 A.D.)

> Bridge Building in Different Dynasties

The period between the Qin (221 B.C.-206 B.C.) and Han (206 B.C.-220 A.D.) dynasties is an important stage of development in the Chinese architectural history. Not only bricks appeared in man-made building materials, craftsmen also invented the arch structure in stones and bricks, which became the foundation for later invention of arch bridges. Iron tools appearing in the Warring States Period improved people's stone processing capabilities so that new stone components such as stone posts, stone beams and stone bridge decks could be added to timber-beam bridges. As a result, stone arch bridges emerged naturally. They are practical, economical and beautiful to look at. They became a landmark in the history of ancient bridge building in China.

等新的构件，石拱桥应运而生。石拱桥不仅实用、经济，而且形式美观，它的出现在中国古代建桥史上具有划时代的意义。

这一时期，在汹涌宽阔的黄河上建起了第一座浮桥——蒲津渡浮桥；在产竹之乡四川又出现了索桥——竹索笮桥。就这样，梁桥、浮桥、索桥和拱桥这四种基本的桥梁形制在中国已全部形成。

During this period the Pujindu Floating Bridge, the first of its kind was built on the turbulent and wide Yellow River and the first suspension bridge the Bamboo Cable Bridge appeared in Sichuan Province, hometown of bamboo production. Thus the four basic bridge structures — beam, floating, suspension and arch — were all established in China.

尾生抱柱

成书于战国时期的道家著作《庄子》中记述了这样一个故事："尾生与女子期于梁下，女子不来，水至不去，抱梁柱而死。"说的是一个叫尾生的男子，和心爱的姑娘约定在一座桥下相会。可姑娘迟迟没来赴约，河水却涨上来了。尾生为了信守诺言，不肯离去，最后竟然抱着桥下的梁柱溺水而亡。这个典故在后来的《史记》《汉书》《艺文类聚》等典籍中都有记载。后人遂用"尾生之信""尾生抱柱"等喻指人坚守信约，忠诚不渝。

Weisheng Holding on to the Bridge Pier

Zhuang Zi, a Taoist work during the Warring States Period tells a story about a man named Weisheng, who planned a date with his girlfriend under a bridge. But the girl never came. The water started to rise. In order to keep his promise, Weisheng refused to leave and eventually drowned while holding on to the bridge pier. This story was also recorded in several classic historical books including *The Historical Records* (*Shi Ji*), *The History of Han* (*Han Shu*) and *Selections of Historical Writings* (*Yiwen Leiju*). Metaphors such as "Weisheng's Trust" or "Weisheng Holding on to the Bridge Pier" all refer to keeping one's promise and remaining loyal to one's friends.

从魏晋开始是古代桥梁发展的鼎盛时期，尤其是隋唐到两宋时期，国力的强盛，社会的安定统一，工商业、运输交通业及科学技术的发达，使中国成为当时世界上最先进的国家。由于东晋以后大量贵族官宦南迁，经济中心自黄河流域移往长江流域，使东南水乡地区的经济得到大发展。而经济和技术的大发展，又反过来刺激了桥梁的

Wei (220-280) and Jin (265-420) dynasties witnessed the development of ancient bridge building at its prime time. Especially from the Sui (581-618) and Tang (618-907) Dynasties to the Song Dynasty(960-1279), China became the most advanced country in the world with strong national power, social stability, peaceful unification, and well-developed industry, commerce, transportation, science and technology. After the East Jin Dynasty (317-420), many imperial officials and their families started to move south. Consequently the economic center began to switch from around the Yellow River Basin to the Yangtze River Basin enabling rapid economic development in southeast of China, a region of many rivers and waterways. Strong economic growth in turn stimulated the development of bridge building in that area. Many world-famous bridges emerged during that time including the Zhaozhou Bridge, the world's oldest open-spandrel stone arch bridge invented by Li Chun, a master stonemason in the Sui Dynasty; Rainbow Bridge (*Hong Qiao*), a timber arch bridge of the post-and-beam structure invented by bridge builders in the Northern Song Dynasty; and Wan'an Bridge built by Cai

上海金泽镇万安桥 （图片提供：FOTOE）
万安桥位于金泽镇北，桥长29米，宽2.6米，建于宋代景定年间。此桥为弧形单孔石拱桥，坡度平缓，跨度大，结构坚固，形式优美，堪称中国造桥史上的奇迹。

Wan'an Bridge in Jinze Town, Shanghai
The Wan'an Bridge is 29m long and 2.6m wide, located in the north of Jinze Town. It was built between 1260 and 1264 during the Song Dynasty. It is a single semicircular arch stone bridge with a large span and a gentle slope. Considered a wonder in the Chinese bridge building history, the bridge has a very solid structure and an elegant profile.

- 《清明上河图》张择端（北宋）【局部】
  《清明上河图》中描绘了一座造型优美的木顶拱桥，横跨在流经北宋都城汴京的汴河之上。此桥规模宏大、结构精巧，宛如飞虹，故名"虹桥"。
  Life along the Bianhe River at the Pure Brightness Festival [Partial] by Zhang Zeduan, Northern Song Dynasty (960-1127)
  This picture depicts an elegant timber arch bridge across the Bian River flowing through Bianjing, the capital of the Northern Song Dynasty. This large bridge has such an exquisite structure that it is described as a flying rainbow, hence the name "Rainbow Bridge".

大发展。因此，这时出现了许多举世瞩目的桥梁，如隋代石匠李春首创的敞肩式石拱桥——赵州桥，北宋人发明的叠梁式木拱桥——虹桥，北宋蔡襄创建的泉州万安桥，等等，这些桥在世界桥梁史上都享有盛誉。纵观中国桥梁史，几乎所有的重大发明和成就，以及能争世界第一的桥梁，都是此时建造的。

Xiang of the Northern Song Dynasty. All these bridges became well-known in the bridge building history of the world. Looking back at the Chinese bridge building history, one cannot help but notice that all important inventions and achievements including the world's first-of-its-kind bridges were built during this period.

送别之桥——灞桥

　　灞桥位于陕西省西安市，是中国现存的已知年代最早、桥面跨度最长的一座大型多孔石拱桥。它始建于隋开皇三年（583年），经唐、五代、宋代的修葺，至元代废毁。桥的总长度达100余米，其桥墩呈船形，长约9.5米，宽约2.5米，残高2.68米，两端有分水尖和石雕吸水兽，拱跨度在5.5米左右，墩下有木桩。此外，在桥体附近还出土了北宋时期维修桥身时所利用的唐代石碑等遗物。灞桥遗址的发现，对于研究中国古代的桥梁建筑史、科技史，以及交通史等，具有重大的意义。

　　西安灞桥是历史上富有诗意的古桥。唐人送客多至灞桥，故又名"销魂桥"。唐朝诗人王之涣（688—742）的诗句："杨柳东风树，青青夹御河。近来攀折苦，应为别离多。"春夏之交，来至灞桥，翠柳低垂，絮花纷飞。折柳赠别，至此黯然。此时此地，诗的氛围和桥的景物水乳交融，产生出一种独特的意境美。

Farewell Bridge—Baqiao Bridge

　　The Baqiao Bridge is situated in Xi'an City, Shaanxi Province, and is the earliest known multi-arch bridge with the longest span in China. It was initially constructed during the Kaihuang Period of the Sui Dynasty in the year 583 and eventually ruined in the Yuan Dynasty after repaired in the Tang Dynasty, Five dynasties and Song Dynasty. The total length of the bridge was over 100m. The bridge had boat-shaped piers, each being 9.5m long, 2.5m wide and 2.68m high. Each of the two bridge ends had a pointed opening to divide the water flow with a stone carved drinking beast. The bridge had a 5.5m span. The bridge piers were supported by wooden piles underneath. Some stone steles used during the bridge repaired in the Northern Song Dynasty were unearthed around the bridge. Discovery of this site has great significance to the research of the bridge building history, history of science and technology, and history of transportation in ancient China.

　　The Baqiao Bridge in Xi'an was a sentimental place in history. People in the Tang Dynasty often bid farewell to their friends at the Baqiao Bridge, hence the name "Melancholy Bridge". Wang Zhihuan (688-742), a well-known poet of the Tang Dynasty described the sentiments at Baqiao Bridge in his poem:

> At the exchange of spring and summer I came to the Baqiao Bridge,
> With willows hanging low and catkins flying around;
> I feel pain breaking willow branches to send you off,
> With much sorrow and many farewells.

　　His poem blends well with the scenery around the bridge, bringing forth a unique artistic beauty.

元、明、清三朝，主要是对一些古桥进行了修缮和改造，并留下了许多修建桥梁的施工说明文献，为后人提供了大量文字资料。此外，也建造完成了一些像明代江西南城县的万年桥、贵州的盘江桥等艰巨工程。同时，在川滇地区兴建

Maintenances and repairs for some of the ancient bridges took place mainly in the Yuan, Ming and Qing dynasties, which left behind many bridge construction specifications providing a large amount of written documents for the later generation. In addition, some difficult projects were completed

- 湖南凤凰虹桥（图片提供：FOTOE）

虹桥又名"风雨楼"，是一座桥上有楼的大石桥，始建于明洪武七年（1374年）。清康熙九年（1670年），虹桥重建过一次，为两台两墩三孔。因桥的两个桥墩呈船形，好像一条雨后彩虹横卧在沱江上，故名为"虹桥"。

Rainbow Bridge in Fenghuang County, Hunan Province

The Rainbow Bridge, also known as the "Rain and Wind Bridge", is a large stone bridge with buildings on the bridge deck. It was originally constructed in 1374 during the Ming Dynasty and rebuilt in 1670 during the Qing Dynasty. It has three arches, two bridge abutments and two boat-shaped bridge piers. The bridge resembles a rainbow across the river, hence the name "Rainbow Bridge".

• 《溪桥策蹇图》戴进（明）【局部】
Painting of Crossing a Small Bridge on Donkeys [Partial] by Dai Jin, Ming Dynasty (1368-1644)

了不少索桥，其建造技术也有所提高。明清时期，许多皇家园林、私人园林中也修建有众多秀美的小桥，其艺术性之高前所未有。

in the Ming Dynasty including the Wannian Bridge in Nancheng County, Jiangxi Province and Panjiang Bridge of Guizhou Province. During the same period, a number of cable suspension bridges were constructed with improved building techniques in Sichuan and Yunnan provinces. In the Ming and Qing dynasties, exquisite and elegant small bridges with artistic designs never seen before were built in many imperial and private gardens.

> 古桥的建筑材料

古人建造桥梁往往因地制宜，就地取材，所以桥梁的建筑材料多种多样，最常见的有木、石、铁、竹、藤等，此外还有特殊的冰桥和盐桥。

木桥是最早的桥梁形式，秦汉以前的桥几乎都是木桥，如最早出现的独木桥、木柱梁桥等。因木材质松易腐，而且受长度和强度的限制，不易在较宽的河流上架桥，也难以牢固耐久。因此从南北朝起，木桥逐渐为木石混合或石构的桥梁所取代。

石桥和砖桥，一般指桥面也是用石或砖料来建造的桥。石桥在中国非常多见，而纯砖构造的桥则极为少见，更多的是砖木或砖石混合构建。春秋战国之际出现了石墩木

> Ancient Bridge Building Materials

Ancient Chinese bridge builders often utilized local materials to adapt to local conditions. Therefore, it is very common to see a good variety of bridge building materials including timber, stone, iron, bamboo and rattan. Additionally there are very special bridges such as the ice bridge and the salt bridge.

Timber bridges are the oldest bridge structure. Before the Qin (221B.C.-206 B.C.) and Han (206 B.C.-220 A.D.) dynasties almost all bridges were timber bridges such as the earliest single-plank bridges or timber beam bridges. However, timber loose and easy to get erosion is also restricted in length and intensity. It is very hard to build a timber bridge on a wide river that can last long. Therefore, after the Southern and Northern dynasties (420-589), timber bridges were replaced

梁的跨空式桥，西汉进一步发展为石柱式石梁桥，东汉则出现了单跨石拱桥。隋代，世界上第一座敞肩式单孔弧形石拱桥——赵州桥建造完成。宋代是大型石桥大发展的时期，出现了像泉州洛阳桥这样长达数里的海上石梁桥，以及像北京卢沟桥这样的大型石拱桥。

竹桥和藤桥主要见于中国南方，尤其是中国的西南地区，一

by bridges of timber and stone structure or of a stone structure.

Stone and brick bridges refer to bridges that have decks also paved with stones or bricks. Stone bridges are very common in China, but bridges built with bricks alone are rare. Most bridges were constructed with both bricks and timbers, or stones and bricks. During the Spring and Autumn Period and Warring States Period (770 B.C.-221 B.C.) trestle bridges of stone piers and timber beams emerged. In the Western Han Dynasty (206 B.C.-25 A.D.) stone beam bridges with stone piers were developed. In the Eastern Han Dynasty (25–220) single-span stone arch bridges came into being. The world's

● 四川上里古镇的二仙桥 (图片提供：FOTOE)
Erxian Bridge in the Ancient Town Shangli, Sichuan Province

- 云南文山壮族村庄中的竹桥
  Bamboo Bridge in a Village Inhabited by Zhuang Ethnic Group in Wenshan, Yunnan Province

- 云南丽江古城的栗木桥
  Chestnut Wood Bridge in Lijiang, Yunnan Province

云南独龙江上的藤桥
Rattan Rope Bridge over Dulong River, Yunnan Province

般建在河面较狭的河流上，作为临时架渡之用。南北朝时称竹质的溜索桥为"笮桥"。后来出现了竹索桥、竹浮桥和竹板桥等。

铁桥在古代包括铁索桥和铁柱桥两种，前者比较多见，约在唐代便已出现。后者属于梁桥类，实为木铁混合桥，极为少见。

盐桥和冰桥诞生于特殊的自然环境中，盐桥主要见于青海的盐湖地区，而冰桥主要在北方寒冷地区。

first open-spandrel single semicircular-arch stone bridge Zhaozhou Bridge was completed in the Sui Dynasty (581-618). The Song Dynasty (960-1279) saw a huge expansion of large-scale stone bridges including the Luoyang Bridge in Quanzhou, a girder stone bridge as long as several miles across the sea, and the Lugou Bridge, a colossal stone arch bridge in Beijing.

Bamboo and rattan bridges are common in South China, especially southwest of China. They were often built over narrow rivers and temporarily used for people to cross the river. In the Southern and Northern dynasties suspension sliding bridges built with bamboo were called *Ze Qiao* meaning a bamboo strip bridge. Later bamboo cable suspension bridges, bamboo floating bridges and bamboo plank bridges also emerged.

There are two types of ancient iron bridges. Iron cable suspension bridges which were first built in the Tang Dynasty (618-907), are common. Iron beam bridges made of both iron and timber are rarely seen.

Salt and ice bridges are products in a special natural environment. Salt bridges are mainly in the salt lake area of Qinghai Province while ice bridges are in the very cold areas in North China.

桥的艺术
Art of Bridges

　　桥是水上架空的建筑，除了特有的实用功能及基本形式外，它的造型不能不受到周围建筑群的影响，需要与人文环境协调一致。另一方面，桥梁又常常架设于林泉胜地，因此要求它要以特有的姿态为优美的自然环境增添风采。作为实用与艺术的融合，中国古代平直的梁桥、凌空的悬索、拱券的圆弧，本身就展现着优美的艺术风姿。而中国古代桥梁的艺术风格，往往体现在其附属建筑和石作雕刻两方面。

A bridge is a structure that spans a body of water. In addition to its special functionalities and a basic structure, the design of a bridge is influenced by the surrounding buildings and must be in harmony with the cultural environment. Often built in the secluded areas are Chinese ancient bridges with unique cultural characteristics so that their presence can add elegance to the enchanting natural environment. Combining practicality and artistry, ancient Chinese bridges demonstrate their original charm through straight and leveled beam bridges, soaring suspension bridges and semicircular arch bridges. The artistic style of Chinese ancient bridges is also presented in their subsidiary structures and stone carvings on the bridge.

> 桥梁的建筑形式

中国地域辽阔，南方和北方地质地貌差异较大，因此各地对建桥技术的要求也各不相同。大约在汉代时，桥梁的四种基本桥型：梁桥、浮桥、索桥、拱桥便已全部产生。

蹬步桥

蹬步桥是人类建筑中最原始的桥梁，即在窄而浅的水中用石块垫起一个接一个略出水面的石蹬，构成一种简陋的"跳墩子"桥，又称"汀步桥"。这类桥虽可达到跨河越谷的目的，但并不具备桥梁架空飞越的特征。这种早期的桥，是道路向桥梁转化的一种过渡形式，是古代桥梁的雏形。

> Bridge Structures

In the vast land of China, there are relatively big differences between southern and northern geological and geomorphological environments, which also impose different requirements for bridge building techniques used in various localities. In the Han Dynasty, all four basic bridge structures: beam, floating, cable suspension and arch, have already emerged.

Stepping Stone Bridges

Stepping stone bridges are considered the most primitive type of bridge structures in the building history of mankind. Basically stepping stones are laid over a narrow and shallow river or a stream to allow pedestrians to cross the water. It is also known as "Tingbu Bridge" meaning crossing the bridge by jumping from one stone step to another. Even though this type of bridges can be used to cross small rivers or valleys, they do not have the capability to support spans or trestles. This early type of ancient bridges represents a transition from roads to bridges.

Floating Bridges

Floating bridges are another type of primitive bridges. The earliest record of floating bridges appeared during the Shang (1600 B.C. -1046 B.C.) and Zhou (1046 B.C. -256 B.C.) dynasties in Chinese history. They were mainly built over wide and deep rivers or places with large up-and-down fluctuations of the water level and impossible to set up stone and timber bridge structures. Floating bridges were made by first

- 水中的蹬步桥
  A Stepping Stone Bridge

浮桥

浮桥也是一种原始的桥梁类型，中国历史上关于浮桥最早的记录出现在商周时期。浮桥主要建于河面过宽及河水过深或涨落起伏较大、一般木石柱梁桥不易架设的地方。浮桥一般是用几十或几百艘船艇（或木筏、竹筏、皮筏）代替桥墩。船艇固定于由棕、麻、竹、铁制成的缆索上，或者用铁锚、铜锚、石锚等设备将船艇固定于江底，而两岸多设柱状构件以系缆索。船艇连结排列于河面上，上铺梁板作为桥面，供人马往来通行。

- 浮桥示意图
  Sketch of a Floating Bridge

对于年水位落差大的季节性河流，则采用拆卸或增装船只的方式，随时调节，以适应水位涨落的落差。浮桥的船艇、桥板与系船的缆绳，须要经常修葺和更换，所以经过岁月变迁的浮桥很少能保留到现在。

- **南浦溪上的万安浮桥**（图片提供：FOTOE）

福建浦城万安乡南浦溪上的浮桥以舟为梁，独具特色。此桥修建于明朝洪武二十五年（1392年），距今有630余年的历史。据史料记载，最初在此修建的是一座木桥，清朝嘉庆十年（1805年），因鉴于此地建桥屡遭洪水毁坏的教训，当地决定改建浮桥。浮桥屡经修复，沿用至今，现长76米，宽3.5米，桥身由12只船组成。

Wan'an Bridge on Nanpu River

The Nanpu River in Wan'an Village, Pucheng City of Fujian Province has a very unique bridge, which uses boats as bridge piers. It was built in the Ming Dynasty 630 years ago. According to historical records, it was originally a timber bridge. In 1805 during the Qing Dynasty, the local people decided to rebuild it into a floating bridge after learning a lesson from flooding that frequently destroyed the bridge. The floating bridge went through many repairs and continues to function today. The bridge is 76m long and 3.5m wide consisting of 12 boats.

arranging dozens or hundreds of boats (or wood rafts, bamboo rafts or canoes) in a row serving as bridge piers. They were then securely attached together with palm or hemp ropes, bamboo cables, or iron chains, and planted on the bottom of the river with iron, bronze or stone anchors. The ropes, cables or chains were fastened with big hooks on posts inserted to the ground on either side of the river. Planks were placed over the boats for traffic by pedestrians and their livestock. In the river where the water level changed frequently, boats could be added or removed at any time according to water-level fluctuations. The boats, planks, cables and chains required frequent maintenance and replacements. Therefore, very few floating bridges could stand erosions and be preserved over the years. When they collapsed, many were replaced by timber or stone beam bridges or stone arch bridges.

Beam Bridges

Beam bridges are the oldest bridge structure in ancient China. It was called the "flat bridge" in ancient times. It has a simple structure and a straight and flat shape. And it is relatively easy to build by simply erecting a wooden or stone

许多浮桥崩毁后，都被木梁桥、石梁桥或石拱桥替代。

梁桥

梁桥是中国古代最早出现的桥梁，古时称做"平桥"。它的结构简单，外形平直，比较容易建造，把木头或石梁架设在河流的两岸，就成了梁桥。在原始社会，中国就

abutment at each end of the river. In the primitive society, single-plank bridges and bridges with several logs laid side by side already appeared in China. Before the Qin Dynasty (221 B.C.-206 B.C.), most of the beam bridges used timber for piers. During the Qin and Han (221 B.C.-220 A.D.) dynasties, bridges built with both stone and timber not only could span relatively wide watercourses, but

- **北京颐和园谐趣园的知鱼桥**

知鱼桥在颐和园的谐趣园中，为七孔平桥形式，桥身贴近水面，让游人可以近距离观赏水中游鱼。

Zhiyu Bridge in the Garden of Harmonious Pleasures (*Xiequ Yuan*), the Summer Palace, in Beijing

The Zhiyu Bridge is in the Garden of Harmonious Pleasures (*Xiequ Yuan*), the Summer Palace. It is a flat bridge with seven openings. The bridge deck is very close to the water, which makes it easy for tourists to watch fish in the pond.

出现了独木桥和数根圆木并排而成的木梁桥。秦代以前的梁桥大多是用木柱做桥墩，随着桩基技术的发展，到了秦汉时期，木石组合的桥梁不但能够跨越较宽大的河道，还能经受住洪波的冲击。后来，为了保护石墩上的木梁，人们在桥上建起了桥屋，即廊桥。这种廊桥最早出现在黄河流域，后多见于南方。

also could stand flooding thanks to the development in the techniques to build bridge foundations. In order to protect beams on stone piers, covered bridges known as corridor bridges began to emerge, first in areas in the Yellow River Basin and later in South China. The most commonly seen are small and medium size stone beam or slab bridges, which are durable and easy to build and maintain.

- 苏州拙政园见山楼前的曲桥

曲桥是梁桥的一种特殊形式，常见于园林中。桥身曲折，一般有三折、四折，乃至九折。其桥面临近水面，栏杆低矮，与水面似分非分，犹有含蓄无尽之意。

The Zigzag Bridge (*Qu Qiao*) in Front of Jianshan Building in the Humble Administrator's Garden of Suzhou

Zigzag bridges are a special kind of beam bridges commonly seen in Chinese gardens. A zigzag bridge can have three, four or even nine zigzag segments. The bridge deck is very close to the water with very low railings giving visitors an interesting sight hard to distinguish the deck surface from the water.

而中小型的石梁桥或石板桥，构造方便，石材耐久，维修省力，是民间最为常见的一种桥形。梁桥若中间无桥墩者，称"单跨梁桥"；若水中有一桥墩，使桥身形成两孔者，便称"双跨梁桥"；若两墩以上者，便称"多跨梁桥"。

If there is no bridge pier, it is called a single-span beam bridge; with one pier and two arches, it is called a "double-span beam bridge"; and with more than two piers, it is called "multiple-span beam bridge".

渭水三桥

坐落在秦代都城咸阳（今陕西咸阳市东）附近的渭水三桥，是古代有名的三座梁桥。三桥包括中渭、东渭和西渭桥，都是多跨木梁木柱桥。其中，中渭桥始建于战国秦昭王时期（前306—前251），全长约525米，宽约13.8米，它由750根木桩组成67个桥墩，68个桥孔，平均每孔跨径为7.72米，在木柱上加盖横梁，再铺上木桥面，桥两侧设雕花栏杆。中间桥孔高而大，两边桥孔低而小，呈八字形，既能通过高大的楼船，又可迅速排除桥面积水。到了汉朝，中渭桥得以重修，又增建了东渭桥和西渭桥，从而并称为"渭水三桥"。

Three Bridges on Weishui River

The Three Bridges on Weishui River located near Xianyang (capital of the Qin Dynasty), Shaanxi Province were very famous beam bridges in ancient times. They are mid-Weiqiao, east-Weiqiao and west-Weiqiao bridges, all multiple-span bridges of timber beams and piers. The mid-Weiqiao Bridge was built during the region of the King Zhao of the State Qin (306B.C.-251 B.C.) with a total length of 525m and a width of 13.8m. It consisted of 67 bridge piers and 68 openings, each having a span of 7.72m. Timber beams were laid across the piers with a wooden deck on top and engraved railings on each side of the bridge. The middle opening was big and high with a smaller opening on each side forming a shape of the Chinese character eight (" 八 "), which not only allowed bigger boats to pass through, but could also get rid of excessive water accumulated on the bridge deck. During the Han Dynasty, the mid-Weiqiao Bridge was rebuilt and at the same time the east-Weiqiao and west-Weiqiao bridges were added, hence the name "Three Bridges on Weishui River".

索桥

　　索桥也称"吊桥""绳桥""悬索桥"等,是用竹索、藤索、铁索等为骨干相拼悬吊起的大桥。中国的索桥主要分布在西南地区,多建于水流湍急而不易立墩的陡岸险谷。其建造方法一般是在两岸建屋,屋内设系绳的立柱和绞绳的转柱,然后用若干粗绳索平铺系紧,再在绳索上横铺木板,有的则在两侧加设一两根绳索作为扶栏。人过索桥时晃晃悠悠,脚下是深谷急流,感觉非常惊险。明代地理学

● 铁索桥
Iron Chain Suspension Bridge

Cable Suspension Bridges

Cable suspension bridges are also called "hanging bridges", "rope bridges" or "dangling bridges". A suspension bridge carries its deck with cables made of bamboo cables, rattan ropes or iron chains hung on vertical suspenders. Most suspension bridges in China were built on perpendicular cliffs or gorges over a rapid watercourse where the construction of bridge piles was impossible. This type of bridge has cables suspended between two houses on each side of the river. Inside each house there are two posts, one standing post to tie the cables and the other turning post capable of releasing or tightening them. Very thick cables are stretched between the posts anchored in the two houses. Planks are laid on the cables as the bridge roadway. Sometimes thick ropes are also used as hand rail chains. Crossing the bridge is a thrilling experience where one can feel the bridge swaying over a deep and raging river. In his travel notes about suspension bridges, the Ming-dynasty geologist Xu Xiake (1587-1641) commented that, "The bridge seems to float in the air from afar, but when you step on it, it is solid and stable." Suspension bridges in China first

惊险的溜索

溜索是索桥的雏形,古代称为"撞",大多以藤或牛皮制成绳索,横悬在两岸陡峭的崖壁上,有平溜和陡溜两种形式。平溜只有一根溜索,基本平直,来往都可以溜渡。但由于溜索中段会自然下垂,所以人溜至中段后往往要用四肢半攀爬地向对岸滑行。而陡溜需要一来一往两根溜索,起点高,终点低,溜渡起来速度快而省力,但容易撞伤,需要格外小心。溜索不仅可以溜渡人,而且还可以溜渡货物、牲畜等。

Thrilling Sliding Ropeways

Sliding ropeways are the original form of suspension bridges. They were called *Zhuang* in ancient China. Most are made of rattan or leather ropes suspended from precipitous cliffs on either side of the river. There are two types of slides: horizontal and steep slides. A horizontal slide only requires one rope for both ways, basically a straightforward operation. However the horizontal ropeway naturally inclines downwards forcing the rider to use all four limbs in a semi-climbing position after midway to slide towards the other end. The steep slide requires one rope for each way with a higher starting point and a lower destination. The steep slide is very fast and effortless, but the rider has to be very careful not to get injured. Sliding ropeways can carry people and transport goods and livestock.

- **怒江上的溜索**

处于西南地区的云南怒江大峡谷,山川险峻、谷深壑长、水流湍急,难以行舟摆渡,自古以来居住在这里的傈僳族、怒族、独龙族等民族的族人就习惯依靠溜索来往和运送物资。

A Sliding Ropeway on Nujiang River

Nujiang Grand Canyon southwest of Yunnan Province has high mountains with steep cliffs, deep valleys and raging waters, which makes it impossible to cross by boat. The Lisu, Nu and Derung and other ethnic groups who have been living here since ancient times still depend on sliding ropeways as a means of transportation of people and goods.

Art of Bridges
桥的艺术

家徐霞客（1587—1641）曾在《徐霞客游记》中评价索桥道："望之飘然，践之则屹然不动。"索桥始见于秦汉时期，现存的著名索桥有明清时期建于四川泸定的泸定桥、都江堰的竹索桥等。

拱桥

拱桥在中国的桥梁史上出现较晚，但拱桥结构一经采用，便得以迅猛发展，成为古桥中最具生命力的一种形式。拱桥有石拱桥、砖拱桥和木拱桥之分，其中砖拱桥极

appeared in the Qin Dynasty (221 B.C. – 206 B.C.). The extant famous suspension bridges include the Luding Bridge of Luding County and the Bamboo Cable Bridge of Dujiangyan in Sichuan Province.

Arch Bridges

Arch bridges emerged relatively late in the Chinese bridge building history. But once its structure was adopted, arch bridges advanced quickly to become the most viable form of ancient bridges. Arch bridges include stone, brick and timber arches, among which brick arches

• 北京颐和园苏州街的单孔石拱桥
A Single-Arch Stone Bridge on Suzhou Street, the Summer Palace, in Beijing

• 苏州拙政园小飞虹

小飞虹这座桥的桥体为三跨石梁，微微拱起，桥的两端与曲廊相连，朱红色的桥栏倒映水中，宛若飞虹，故名。它不仅是连接水面和陆地的通道，而且构成了以桥为中心的独特景观。

Small Flying Rainbow Bridge in the Humble Administrator's Garden (*Zhuozheng Yuan*), Suzhou City

The Small Flying Rainbow Bridge is a slightly-arched stone beam bridge with three spans. The two ends of the bridge are connected to the zigzagged corridors. The reflection of the red railings on the water resembles a rainbow, hence the name "Small Flying Rainbow Bridge". It not only functions as a walkway connecting the water to the land, but also becomes a unique sight with the bridge as the focus.

少见，常见的是石拱桥。拱桥又有单拱、双拱、多拱之分，拱的多少视河的宽度而定。多拱桥一般正中的拱特别高大，而两边的拱则略小。依拱的形状不同，拱桥又有五边、半圆、尖拱、坦拱之分。石拱桥桥面一般铺石板，桥边做石栏

are very rare. Commonly seen are stone arch bridges. An arch bridge can have a single arch, double arches or multiple arches. The number of arches for a bridge depends on the width of the river. A multiple-arch bridge usually consists of a very high arch in the middle and smaller arches on either side. The shape

杆。拱桥最早的形象出现在东汉的画像砖上。中国现存最早且最具代表性的石拱桥，要数隋代李春设计建造的赵州桥。

of the arch can be pentagonal, semicircle, pointed or leveled. The bridge deck of a stone arch bridge is usually paved with stone slabs with stone railings. The image of an arch bridge first appeared in a painted tile in the Eastern Han Dynasty (25-220). Among the extant arch bridges in China today, the oldest and the most representative of stone arch bridges is the Zhaozhou Bridge designed and built by Li Chun of the Sui Dynasty (581-618).

- 《玉带桥诗意图》徐扬（清）
Poetic Painting of the Jade Belt Bridge by Xu Yang, Qing Dynasty (1616-1911)

> 桥梁的装饰

中国桥梁的附属建筑和部件，如桥栏、桥亭、桥联、桥碑、桥头建筑，都是能工巧匠和文人雅士一展身手的地方，绘画、书法、雕塑、文学等都可以在桥梁的设计装饰上得到充分的展示。

桥栏

桥栏是桥梁上部结构中的一个构件，既能保护行人安全，又起到

> Bridge Decorations

Ancient Chinese bridges usually comprise various supplementary buildings or components such as bridge railings, bridge pavilions, bridge couplets, bridge steles and bridgehead structures, all of which became a showplace for master craftsmen, scholars and artists to demonstrate their paintings, calligraphies, sculptures and literary works.

Bridge Railings

The Bridge railing is a component in

- **石拱桥边的镇水兽**

古桥桥头常有石雕神兽，古人将其作为古桥的守护神，相信它能威震四方，战胜各种邪恶，保证古桥的安全。镇水兽的造型千姿百态。古代在举行古桥启用仪式时，往往要给桥头神兽挂红披彩。

Mythical Beasts on a Stone Arch Bridge

Stone carved mythical beasts are commonly seen at the bridgehead of a Chinese ancient bridge. They were regarded by ancient Chinese as sacred guardians to defeat all kinds of evils and protect the safety of the bridge. They were carved into a great variety of shapes and styles. They were usually dressed up in red in the ceremony to celebrate the completion of a bridge in the past.

增加桥梁整体强度的作用。桥栏一般由栏板、望柱和抱鼓石组成。中国古桥桥栏的设计首先注重安全性，石桥的桥栏往往使用体量较大的石板。同时，桥栏与桥梁主体高度协调，形成和谐的艺术效果。许多桥梁采用长方形栏板，按桥型和落坡走势安装，形成桥拱曲线和桥栏直线的有机结合。

桥栏的栏板、望柱、抱鼓上往

the upper structure of a bridge to protect pedestrians and increase the overall strength of the bridge as well. A bridge rail usually consists of a parapet panel, a stone post and a round stone structure called Baogu stone meaning embracing the drum stone. The railings of ancient Chinese bridges were often made of heavy and large stone slates for the safety of pedestrians. At the same time attention was also given to the artistic effect of the balance and coordination between the rails and the bridge body height. Many bridges installed rectangular parapet panels according to the shape of the bridge and the deck slope in order to achieve a natural integration of the curved shape of the bridge and the straight lines of the bridge railings.

• 汉白玉石拱桥的栏杆
White Marble Railings of a Stone Arch Bridge

望柱 Posts

栏板 Railing Panels

寻杖 Barriers

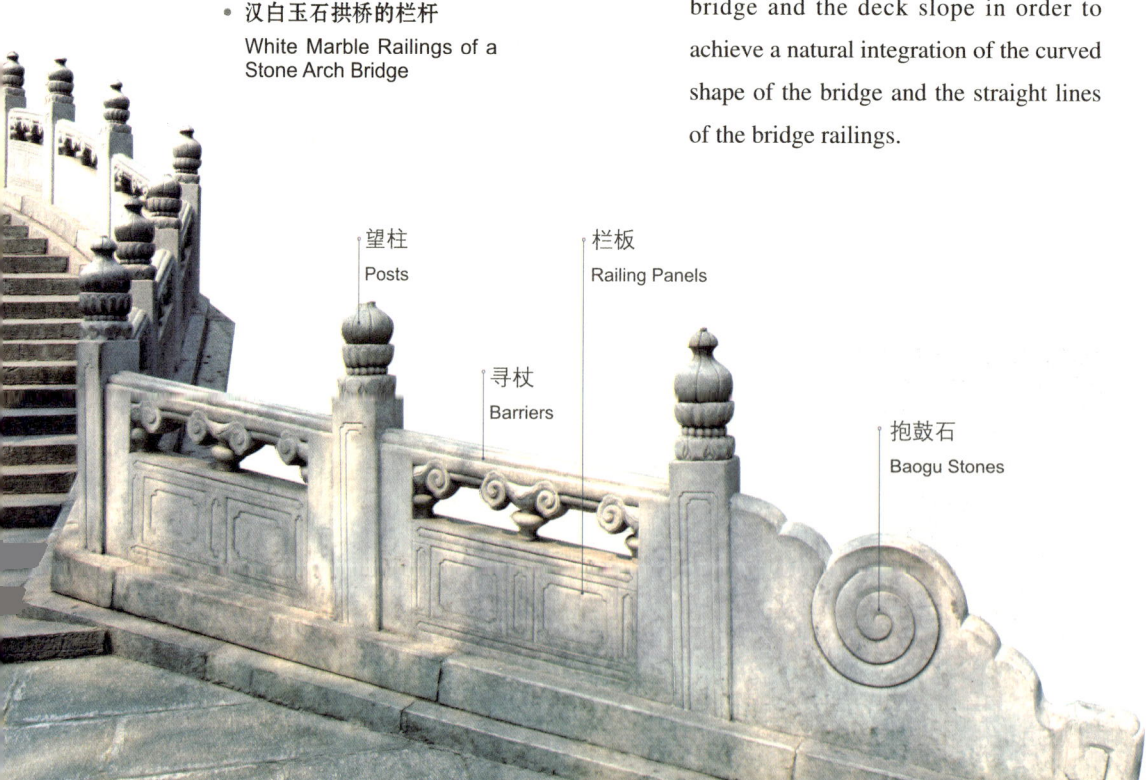

抱鼓石 Baogu Stones

- **湖南德夯接龙桥**（图片提供：FOTOE）

接龙桥是一座半圆形的石拱桥，桥头两端接着巨大青石板砌成的石板路，连起了夯峡溪两岸的苗寨。"接龙"之名有接济、调节水源的寓意。

Receiving Loong Bridge (*Jielong Qiao*), Dehang, Hunan Province

The Receiving Loong Bridge is a semicircular stone arch bridge connecting to a walkway paved with huge flagstone slabs at each end of the bridge and also connecting the Miao villages on both sides of the Hangxian River. Receiving Loong means to get the loong's help in regulating the water source.

往还装饰有多种造型和图案，都是古代雕刻艺术品。最具代表性的桥栏石雕造型和图案有龙、镇水兽、鹿、麒麟、蝙蝠、暗八仙、鲤鱼跳龙门等。

Parapet panels, railing posts and round Baogu stones are often carved in patterns and shapes representing ancient Chinese sculpting art. The most representative of the bridge railing

• 浙江杭州胡雪岩故居内的晴雨亭桥
Qingyu Pavilion Bridge in Hu Xueyan's Residence in Hangzhou City, Zhejiang Province

桥亭

中国古桥的桥头常建有桥亭。作为古桥的配套设施，桥亭既有供过往行人歇息的功能，又有美化古桥、平衡古桥布局的作用。古石桥的桥亭大多为石亭，建筑材料质地与桥协调，造型美观。在一些地方，如江南地区，在古代往

carvings include loongs, kylin, and bats as well as instruments of the eight immortals and images of carps jumping over a loong gate.

Bridge Pavilions

Pavilions were often built at the bridgeheads of Chinese ancient bridges. As a complementary structure for the bridge, a pavilion provides a rest place for

往还有在桥亭为来往行人免费施茶的传统。

牌楼

不少古桥在桥头立有石牌楼，既增加了古桥的美感，又加强了古桥的威严意味。因为造有牌楼的古桥往往非同一般，或是通向官衙，或是名人所造，也有的是皇帝亲自降旨建造的桥。牌楼是

北京颐和园谐趣园知鱼桥石牌楼
Stone Gateway of the Zhiyu Bridge in the Garden of Harmonious Pleasures, the Summer Palace, in Beijing

pedestrians and also beautifies the entire bridge layout. Most of them are stone pavilions in a beautiful profile consistent with the bridge's building materials. In some places south of the Yangtze River, there used to be a custom to serve free tea to pedestrians in bridge pavilions.

Gateways (*Pailou*)

Many ancient bridges have a gateway set up at the bridgehead adding an aesthetic and majestic touch to the bridge. Unlike other ordinary ancient bridges, most bridges with a gateway were connected to a passageway to government buildings, or constructed by notable personalities or by a decree from the emperor himself. The gateway was considered the highest form of bridgehead structures, which usually used multiple stone carving techniques such as embossment and engraving with exquisite and complex patterns of a higher artistic level.

Bridge Steles

There are different kinds of bridge steles. Monumental steles were erected at the bridgehead after the bridge was built to display the history of the bridge, the building and repair processes. Other

桥头建筑中规格最高的一种，一般采用浮雕、透雕等多种石雕手法，饰有精美复杂的图案，艺术水平较高。

桥碑

古桥的桥碑有多种类型，一类是纪念型桥碑，即桥建成后，立碑于桥头，记述桥史和建桥、修桥过程。第二类是刻有名人题写的桥名和其他特定碑文的桥碑，它们往往成为古桥的一道景观。桥碑上高超的书法、优美的碑文是桥梁美的重要元素。

bridge steles have inscriptions of their names by celebrities or of certain specific writings. These steles usually became tourist attractions for the ancient bridges. The superb calligraphy and refined inscriptions on these steles have become an important element to demonstrate the beauty of the ancient bridges.

- 卢沟桥桥头的康熙重修卢沟桥碑
  The Renovation of the Lugou Bridge Stele by Emperor Kangxi of the Qing Dynasty

各地名桥
Famous Bridges

　　在中华大地上留存至今的古桥难以胜数，受所在地的影响，各地的桥梁都形成了各自相对独立的风格和特色。

There are numerous extant ancient bridges in the vast land of China. Bridges in different regions have their own unique characteristics and features influenced by the local culture.

中国北方四季分明，一年中河水的流量变化很大，夏季多洪水，冬、春季有寒冰，因此修筑的桥梁需要十分稳固，方能抗洪、抗冰。北方中原地区，地势较为平坦，河流水域较少，人们运输物资多依赖骡马大车或手推板车，所以北方的桥梁大都宽大结实，以石梁桥、石

North China has distinct four seasons. The river water flow varies greatly in a year with a lot of flooding in the summer and icy water in the spring. Therefore bridges must be very strong and secure to resist floods and ice. The northern central plains have relatively flat terrains with relatively fewer waterways. In ancient China transportation mainly depended

• 颐和园后溪河三孔石桥
Three-Hole Stone Bridge on Houxi River, the Summer Palace

拱桥为主，显得稳重、雄伟而富有气势。中国南方雨量充沛，河水水位也比较平稳，因此修建的桥梁结构较为轻盈，装饰精美，显得玲珑秀美，富有韵致。西南地区多高山峡谷，岸陡水急，无论是在水中修筑桥墩，还是修筑单跨的单跨梁桥或拱桥，都十分困难。于是人们便因地制宜，用藤条、竹索、铁索架设了许多飞渡而过的索桥。

on wagons pulled by mules or horses and small two-wheel carts pushed by people. In the north, there are mostly stone beam or stone arch bridges, usually wide and enduring with a solid and magnificent appearance. South China enjoys abundant rainfalls and a relatively stable river water level. As a result, the bridge structures are usually light with refined decorations and an elegant look. Regions in Southwest China have numerous high mountains and valleys. Steep river banks and rapid water flow make it very difficult to build bridge piers, single-span bridges or arch bridges in the water. Therefore many suspension bridges of rattan ropes, bamboo cables and iron chains were built to adapt to local conditions.

> 金水桥

中国古代皇家建筑的正门外常常设有御沟，名"金水河"，河上架的桥就称为"金水桥"。这种桥是区分内外庭的界线，同时也有彰显皇家气势的作用。现存的金水桥，以明清皇宫（现北京故宫）的为最佳。

故宫金水桥分为内金水桥和外金水桥。外金水桥位于天安门前面，始建于明永乐十五年（1417年），重建于清康熙二十九年（1690年），共计七座，中间五座分别与天安门城楼的五个门洞相对应。这七座桥在使用对象上各有不同，正中的一座最为宽大，长23.15米，宽8.55米，为皇帝一人专用，称为"御路桥"；御路桥左右的桥宽5.78米，叫"王公桥"，是供宗室

> Golden Water Bridges (*Jinshui Qiao*)

Imperial buildings in ancient China often have a wide moat called "Golden Water River" built outside of the front gate. Bridges on this river are called "Golden Water Bridges" used to divide the inner and outer courts for the purpose of demonstrating the imposing presence of the imperial palace. The best extant Golden Water Bridges are those built for the palace of the Ming and Qing dynasties (now the Beijing Forbidden City).

The Golden Water Bridges in the Forbidden City are divided into Inner and Outer Golden Water Bridges. The Outer Golden Water Bridges, located in front of the Tian'anmen Square, were built originally in 1417 during the Ming Dynasty and rebuilt in 1690 during the Qing Dynasty. There are a total of 7 bridges with 5 bridges in the middle

亲王们通行的；王公桥外侧的桥较窄，宽4.55米，叫"品级桥"，供三品及以上文武官员通行；而最外侧的两座桥叫"公生桥"，供四品及以下官员、兵弁、夫役来往使用。各桥的建筑装饰也各不一样，御路桥的栏杆柱头上雕刻的是蟠龙纹，下衬云板，其余四座的白石栏杆上皆雕刻荷花纹，反映出古代社会森严的等级制度。

内金水桥位于故宫内太和门前的内金水河上，是五座并列单孔

corresponding to the 5 gates of the Tian'anmen Tower. Each of the 7 bridges has its own functionality. The one in the very center is the largest, 23.15m long and 8.55m wide, reserved solely for the emperor himself. It was called the "Imperial Path Bridge". The bridges on either side of the Imperial Path Bridge were called "Prince and Duke Bridges" with a width of 5.78m reserved for imperial family members. The bridges next to the two Prince and Duke Bridges could only be used by high-ranking

- 内金水桥的汉白玉栏杆

White Marble Railings of the Inner Golden Water Bridges

拱券式的汉白玉石桥。这五座桥随着弯曲如弓的金水河河道也成弧形排列，桥的规格制式和外金水桥相同。

　　内外金水桥的桥面均稍有坡度，中间出现拱面，而且桥身中间窄，两端宽。这种变化多姿、起伏曲折的线条，似"蹑玉桥之长虹"，与线条方正、高大雄伟的宫殿建筑相得益彰。

• 天安门前的外金水桥
Outer Golden Water Bridges in Front of Tian'anmen

imperial civil and military officials. The most outer bridges were Bridges of Commoners used by lower-ranking imperial officials, soldiers and laborers. Decorations on each bridge are different. The rails on the bridge reserved solely for the emperor have carved coiling loongs on clouds. The other 4 bridges for imperial families and officials have white stone railings carved with lotus flowers. All these reflect the rigidly stratified class system of the ancient society.

　　In front of the Gate of Supreme Harmony (*Taihe Men*) are the Inner Golden Water Bridges, 5 white marble single-span arch bridges arranged in a semicircle across the meandering Inner Golden Water Rivers. They have the same size and style as the Outer Golden Water Bridges.

　　Both the decks of the Inner Golden Water Bridges and the Outer Golden Water Bridge have a gentle slope. The bridges has a narrower width in the center and wider bridge ends. The curving shape of the bridge deck looks like a rainbow across a jade bridge complementary to the square-shape majestic imperial palace halls.

> 断虹桥

断虹桥位于北京故宫太和门和武英殿之间的金水河上，是一座单孔汉白玉石拱桥，南北走向，全长18.7米，通宽9.2米，呈两头宽、中间细的喇叭腰形。断虹桥两侧共有望柱20根，每侧10根，两两相对，每根望柱底部雕刻一圈连珠莲花须弥座，座顶雕刻形态各异的石狮，有的石狮身上还刻有小狮，造型生动，活泼可爱，大小共34只。望柱间嵌有石栏板，两边共有18块，每块栏板的上部透雕莲花盆景，下部是双龙追逐嬉戏牡丹宝相花的浮雕图案。桥两头各有两只披头散发的石兽。石兽整体雕刻线条流畅，肌体健硕，头披毛发，怒发冲冠，双目圆睁，炯炯有神，动感十足。

> Broken Rainbow Bridge (*Duanhong Qiao*)

The Broken Rainbow Bridge is a white marble single-arch bridge located on the Golden Water River between the Gate of Supreme Harmony (*Taihe Men*) and the Hall of Martial Valor (*Wuying Dian*). It has a width of 9.2m and a length of 18.7m from south to north, narrower in the middle and wider on both ends. There are 20 stone posts supporting the railings, 10 on each side opposite each other and each carved with a circle of Sumeru lotus flowers. At the top of the railing posts stand 34 crarved stone lions in different moods and postures. Some stone lions have a lovely baby lion on their bodies. There are 18 railing panels, each having an engraved lotus bonsai in the upper part and two embossed loongs playing with peonies in the lower part. On each bridgehead there are two strongly-built stone beasts with disheveled hair and wide-opened eyes showing off their vitality.

- 故宫断虹桥

据考证，断虹桥始建于元代，原是元皇宫崇天门外的周桥。断虹桥下的河流也是利用了元代旧有的河道。据记载，元代的周桥原有"三虹"（在古代，"虹"的意思主要是虹形桥梁，每一道桥梁称为"一虹"）。明永乐年间重修皇宫后，周桥已经不在皇城正门，也不能保留其三虹的规格，于是加以改动，截去两虹，留其一虹，所以改称"断虹"。

Broken Rainbow Bridge in the Forbidden City

According to historical research, the Broken Rainbow Bridge was the original Zhouqiao Bridge built in the Yuan Dynasty (1206-1368) outside of the Chongtian Gate of the Yuan-dynasty imperial palace. The river around the Broken Rainbow Bridge is also part of the old watercourse of the Yuan Dynasty. Historical records show that the original Zhouqiao Bridge had three so-called "rainbows". (In the past, *Hong*, meaning rainbow, represented rainbow-shaped bridge beam). In the Ming Dynasty, the imperial palace was rebuilt and the old Zhouqiao Bridge was no longer located at the front gate of the imperial palace. As a result, the bridge was not allowed to keep the original three-rainbow style. Two rainbow-style beams were removed, hence the name "Broken Rainbow Bridge".

> 金鳌玉蝀桥

金鳌玉蝀桥原名"金海桥",又叫"御河桥",位于北京北海公园的团城脚下,横跨于北海与中海之间,俗称"北海大桥"。此桥始建于元代至元元年(1264年),最初是一座木桥。明弘治二年(1489

> Bridge of Golden Turtle and Jade Rainbow (*Jin'ao Yudong Qiao*)

The Bridge of Golden Turtle and Jade Rainbow, originally named "Golden Sea Bridge" and "Imperial River Bridge", is located at the foot of the Round City

- 金鳌玉蝀桥桥西的三座大门及牌楼旧照(民国)
  An Old Photo of Three Gates and One Gateway to the West of Bridge of Golden Turtle and Jade Rainbow, Photoed in Minguo Period (1912-1949)

年)五月,木桥改建为石桥,桥东西两端各建一座木牌坊,西牌坊上书"金鳌"二字,东牌坊书"玉蝀"二字,因此这座桥又称"金鳌玉蝀"桥。旧时的金鳌玉蝀桥总长156.73米,桥宽9.48米,为九孔拱券式石桥,每个石拱券顶都雕有一尊吸水兽头。桥两侧原是汉白玉石栏,整个桥身如同一条洁白无瑕的玉带。

20世纪50年代,为了适应交通发展的需要,金鳌玉蝀桥得以改建。改建后的大桥保持了原桥的风格,桥面加宽,坡度减小,桥面改为沥青路面,桥下只保留中间的桥洞流水畅通,其余的桥洞均堵死,只为装饰之用。

• 北海金鳌玉蝀桥(图片提供:FOTOE)
Bridge of Golden Turtle and Jade Rainbow in Beihai Park

(*Tuan Cheng*) across the north and middle part of the Beihai Park, Beijing. It is commonly known as the Big Bridge of Beihai (*Beihai Daqiao*). It was originally a timber bridge constructed in 1264 during the Yuan Dynasty. In May 1489 the timber bridge was rebuilt into a stone bridge. A wooden gateway stands on each end of the bridge; the one in the west is inscribed with *Jin'ao* (Golden Turtle) and the one in the east is inscribed with *Yudong* (Jade Rainbow), hence the name Bridge of Golden Turtle and Jade Rainbow. The original bridge was 156.73m long and 9.48m wide with nine arches. Each of the arch crowns has a carved head of a mythical beast. The bridge railings were originally made of white marbles, which made the bridge look like a flawless white jade belt.

In the 1950s, the bridge was renovated in order to meet the needs of transportation development. The new bridge retained the original architectural style, increased the width of the bridge deck, and decreased the bridge slope. The deck was paved with asphalt. Only one arch is open today to allow water to pass, and the other arches are blocked and used mainly for decorations.

> 堆云积翠桥

堆云积翠桥坐落在北京北海公园内，又名"永安桥"。此桥的前身是建于元代至元三年（1266年）的一座单孔木桥。当时桥两端以石料砌成护岸，中间铺木板装木栏杆。清乾隆八年（1743年）将此桥改建为三曲折的三孔石拱桥，桥长85米，宽7.6米，两侧有汉白玉望柱48根。桥南桥北有"堆云""积翠"两座牌坊，所以桥名定为"堆云积翠桥"。又因桥在永安寺正门的南边，又称"永安桥"。

此桥建成后，将北海南岸的团城城门和白塔所在的琼岛上的永安寺寺门巧妙地连接起来，构成了进入公园后的第一道风景。每到夏季，桥东侧的大片荷塘荷花盛开，

> Bridge of Cloud Gathering and Greens Overlapping (Duiyun Jicui Qiao)

Bridge of Cloud Gathering and Greens Overlapping also known as Yong'an Bridge, is located inside the Beihai Park in Beijing. It was originally a single-arch timber bridge built in 1266 during the Yuan Dynasty with a plank bridge deck and timber railing with the two ends of the bridge extending to the stone embankments of the river. In 1743 during the Qing Dynasty the bridge was rebuilt into a three-arch stone bridge at 85m long and 7.6m wide with a total of 48 white marble railing posts on each side. Two gateways inscribed with *Duiyun* (cloud gathering) and *Jicui* (greens overlapping) stand at the southern and northern end of the bridge, hence the name "Bridge of Cloud Gathering and Greens Overlapping". The bridge is also called

北海堆云积翠桥
Bridge of Cloud Gathering and Greens Overlapping Bridge, in Beihai Park

粉红色的荷花和大桥、白塔相映成趣，令人心旷神怡。

- 桥南端的"积翠"牌坊
The Gateway Inscribed with "Greens Overlapping" at the Southern End of the Bridge

Yong'an Bridge since it is located south of the front gate of the Yong'an Temple.

After its completion, this bridge became the first sight upon entering the Beihai Park masterfully linking the Round City gate with the gate of the Yong'an Temple on the island where the white pagoda is situated. In summer, it is an enchanting view of pink lotus flowers blossoming under the big bridge with the white pagoda in the background.

> 十七孔桥

　　十七孔桥坐落在北京颐和园内宽阔的昆明湖上，整体桥长150米，宽8米，因由17个桥洞组成而得名，是园内最大的一座石桥。十七孔桥西连南湖岛，东接廓如亭，飞跨于东堤和南湖岛之间，不但是前往南

> Seventeen-Arch Bridge
(Shiqikong Qiao)

The Seventeen-Arch Bridge is located on the Kunming Lake in the Summer Palace, Beijing. It is 150m long and 8m wide. Named after the seventeen arches, it is the biggest bridge in the park across the East Causeway and the South Lake

湖岛的唯一通道，而且是湖区的一个重要景点。

十七孔桥建于清乾隆年间，桥上所有的匾联均为清代乾隆皇帝所撰写。桥的南端横联上刻有"修蝀凌波"四个字，形容十七孔桥如同一道彩虹，飞架于碧波之上。桥的北端横联有"灵鼍偃月"四个字，又把十七孔桥比喻成水中神兽，横卧水中呈半月状。十七个桥洞从中间最大的桥洞向两端数去都是"九"，体现出古人对"九"的尊崇。

Island connecting the island to the west and Kuoru Pavilion to the east. It is the only route to the South Lake Island and a major tourist attraction in the park.

The Seventeen-Arch Bridge was built between 1736 and 1795 during the reign of Emperor Qianlong in the Qing Dynasty. All couplets and tablets on the bridge were inscribed by Emperor Qianlong. The horizontal tablet at the southern end of the bridge is inscribed with four Chinese characters *Xiu Dong Ling Bo* describing the bridge's resemblance to a colorful

- 颐和园十七孔桥

造型优美的十七孔桥将昆明湖的水面分出层次，千亩碧波尽收眼底的空旷感，因为此桥的出现而消弭无踪，这堪称园林设计者的神来之笔。

Seventeen-Arch Bridge in the Summer Palace

The elegant Seventeen-Arch Bridge is a masterpiece of the imperial garden designers. When looking from afar, the bridge seems to separate the water in the Kunming Lake into different layers making the feeling of the lake's vastness disappear.

十七孔桥东端的廊如亭

廊如亭是一座八角形的大亭子,俗称"八方亭",建于清乾隆年间。中国园林中的亭子多小巧玲珑,但廊如亭却是例外,它的面积有130多平方米,体量之宏堪称全国之冠。雄浑气派的廊如亭由十七孔桥与南湖岛相连接。十七孔桥就像一根扁担挑起两大景物,形成从万寿山向昆明湖南望的主要景观。

Kuoru Pavilion at the East End of the Bridge

Built during the reign of Emperor Qianlong of the Qing Dynasty, Kuoru Pavilion (meaning spacious pavilion) is in an octangle shape, commonly known as the "Pavilion of Eight Sides". Most of the pavilions in Chinese gardens are small and delicate. But this one is an exception covering an area of over 130 square meters, the largest of its kind in the whole country. This magnificent pavilion connects to the South Lake Island via the Seventeen-Arch Bridge as if a pole carried two big scenic objects. It is a major attraction on the Kunming Lake when viewing south from the Longevity Hill(*Wanshou Shan*).

- 十七孔桥上的狮子

Stone Lions on the Seventeen-Arch Bridge

rainbow over the water. The horizontal tablet at the northern end of the bridge is inscribed with another four Chinese characters *Ling Tuo Yan Yue* personifying the bridge in the form of a beast lying in the water in a half-moon shape. Counting from the biggest arch in the middle there are nine arches on each side, which demonstrates the reverence for the double nine number by ancient Chinese.

The railings on each side of the bridge are supported by 128 white stone

十七孔桥两边的白石栏杆共有128根望柱，每根望柱上都雕刻着精美的石狮，大小共544只，有的母子相抱，有的玩耍嬉闹，有的你追我赶，个个惟妙惟肖。两端桥头各有两只石刻异兽，形象威猛异常，极为生动。

posts, on which stand a total of 544 small and big exquisite stone lions showing mother lions embracing baby lions or lions running after each other. Each bridgehead has two stone carved mythical beasts with a mighty and vivid image.

- 十七孔桥桥头雕塑
  Sculptures on the Bridgehead of the Seventeen-Arch Bridge

> 绣漪桥

绣漪桥建造于1750年，位于北京颐和园南如意门内，地处昆明湖与长河、东堤与西堤的交界处。清代帝后来颐和园游玩时，经常从西

> Colorful Ripples Bridge (Xiuyi Qiao)

The Colorful Ripples Bridge, built in 1750, is located near the South Ruyi Gate of the Summer Place right at the junction between the Kunming Lake and the Long River, and between the East and the West Causeways. When emperors and

- 颐和园绣漪桥
  Colorful Ripples Bridge in the Summer Palace

直门外上船，经长河从绣漪桥下进入昆明湖，故而此桥素有"昆明湖第一桥"之称。为便于行船，绣漪桥建成高拱形的单孔桥，桥身精美华丽。桥全长44.8米，宽5.8米，桥堍外口宽19米，设计和建造都十分讲究。桥洞上方有"绣漪桥"桥额，两侧镌刻有对联，为清代乾隆帝御笔亲题。

empresses came to the Summer Palace by boat, they would pass under this bridge via the Long River into the Kunming Lake making the bridge known as the "No. 1 Bridge on the Kunming Lake". This tall single-arch bridge is 44.8m long and 5.8m wide with a 19m width at the bridgehead demonstrating its delicate and careful design and construction. The name of the bridge is inscribed on the arch crown with a couplet carved on each side, all personally written by Emperor Qianlong.

颐和园西堤六桥

颐和园昆明湖上的西堤是仿照杭州西湖的苏堤而建，从颐和园北如意门进去，就是西堤的北起点，向东南方向蜿蜒5公里，直达南端与东堤汇合，有六座桥点缀其间。这六座桥从北到南依次为界湖桥、豳风桥、玉带桥、镜桥、练桥和柳桥，合称"西堤六桥"。

Six Bridges on the Summer Palace West Causeway

The West Causeway is modeled on the Su Causeway of the West Lake in Hangzhou City. Its northern end starts from the North Ruyi Gate of the Summer Palace, extends 5 kilometers to the southeast and connects with the East Causeway in the southern end. The entire West Causeway is dotted by six bridges from north to south: Lake-Dividing Bridge (*Jiehu Qiao*), Bridge of Pastoral Poems (*Binfeng Qiao*), Jade Belt Bridge (*Yudai Qiao*), Mirror Bridge (*Jing Qiao*), Silk Bridge (*Lian Qiao*) and Willow Bridge (*Liu Qiao*). Collectively they are referred to as "the Six Bridges on the West Causeway".

界湖桥

界湖桥位于西堤的最北端，原名柳桥。此桥南北方向坐落，桥下有三个方形桥洞，桥上原有木构桥亭，1860年第二次鸦片战争中被英法联军焚毁。1886年重修颐和园时，未重建桥亭。以其分界昆明湖内外湖与后溪河，改名"界湖桥"。

Lake-Dividing Bridge *(Jiehu Qiao)*

Situated at the very northern end of the West Causeway, the bridge was originally named "Willow Bridge". The bridge faces south and has three square openings. It used to have on top a wooden pavilion, which was destroyed in the fire set by the Anglo-French Allied Forces in the Second Opium War in 1860. During the Summer Palace's reconstruction in 1886, the pavilion was not rebuilt and the bridge was renamed "Lake-Dividing Bridge" because of its position, which divides the inner and outer Kunming Lake from the Houxi River.

豳风桥

豳（音"宾"）风桥在界湖桥南。桥西原有"耕织图"等与农事有关的景致，所以，乾隆帝将它命名为"桑苎桥"。1860年，桑苎桥被英法联军烧毁。1886年，慈禧太后重建颐和园时将其改名为"豳风桥"。"豳风"是《诗经》十五国风之一，其中多描写百姓农耕生活的诗歌，故引经据典用作桥名。豳风桥的桥身与界湖桥相比尺寸略小，桥洞造型也稍有不同，中间的桥洞为方形，两边为圆形。

Bridge of Pastoral Poems *(Binfeng Qiao)*

This bridge is situated to the south of the Lake-Dividing Bridge. It was originally named the Mulberry and Ramie Bridge by Emperor Qianlong of the Qing Dynasty because of some farmland scenery to the west of the bridge. In 1860 it was destroyed in the fire set by the Anglo-French Allied Forces. In 1886 Empress Dowager Cixi changed its name to Bridge of Pastoral Poems, which came from *The Book of Songs* about rural farming life in ancient China. This bridge is a little smaller than the Lake-Dividing Bridge and also relatively different in style with a square opening in the center and two round arches on each side.

各地名桥 Famous Bridges

- 玉带桥

玉带桥为单孔高拱形石桥，桥身高高拱起，形似古人佩饰的玉带，因此得名。玉带桥桥拱高而薄，弧形线条十分流畅，半圆的桥洞与水中的倒影构成一轮透明的圆月，景象十分动人。

Jade Belt Bridge *(Yudai Qiao)*

The Jade Belt Bridge is a single open high arch stone bridge. It was named after its high arch which resembles the jade belt worn by ancient Chinese. This slender and high-arch bridge displays an enchanting image of a smooth curved line with the semicircular arch constituting a transparent full-moon reflection in the water at night.

- 镜桥

镜桥在玉带桥南，为一平两坡式，桥下有方形桥孔，桥上有八方重檐攒尖式的桥亭。"镜桥"之名取自唐代诗人李白"两水夹明镜，双桥落彩虹"的诗句。

Mirror Bridge *(Jing Qiao)*

Situated to the south of the Jade Belt Bridge, the Mirror Bridge has a so-called "one level surface with two slopes" style. It has a square opening below and an octagonal-shaped pavilion with pointed roof and double eaves on the bridge deck. The bridge was named after a verse from a poem by Li Bai (701-762) of the Tang Dynasty, "A bright mirror between two rivers, a rainbow falls over two bridges".

- 练桥

练桥为一孔桥，桥上有四方形重檐攒尖顶桥亭。此处视野开阔，站在桥上，南湖岛、十七孔桥、佛香阁建筑群等环桥景致都能一一收入眼中。

Silk Bridge *(Lian Qiao)*

The Silk Bridge is a single-arch bridge with a square-shaped pavilion of double eaves and pointed roof on the bridge deck. Standing on the bridge, one can enjoy a broad view of the South Lake Island, the Seventeen-Arch Bridge and the Tower of the Buddhist Incense building complex.

● 柳桥

柳桥在西堤南端，为屋桥形式，桥身较高，有一方、四圆五个桥洞，桥身上建有一座四方桥亭。柳桥与西堤一并镶嵌在湖水之中，背景是玉泉山宝塔，整体景色非常壮丽，为昆明湖一大景观。原名界湖桥，重建颐和园时，与北端的柳桥易名。

Willow Bridge *(Liu Qiao)*

Situated at the southern end of the West Causeway, the relatively higher Willow Bridge has one square opening in the middle with two arches on each side and a square-shaped pavilion on top. It is one of the major sights on the Kunming Lake with the Willow Bridge and the West Causeway on the lake against the Pagoda of Jade Spring Hills in the background. The bridge was originally named "Lake-Dividing Bridge", but was interchanged name with the very northern Willow Bridge when the Summer Palace was reconstructed.

> 卢沟桥

卢沟桥位于北京市西南约15千米的永定河上，是北京现存最古老的联拱石桥。桥全长266.5米，宽约7.5米，最宽处可达9.3米。有桥墩10座，共11个桥孔，整个桥身都是石体结构，关键部位有银锭铁榫连接。

> Lugou Bridge

The Lugou Bridge is located about 15 kilometers southwest of Beijing on the Yongding River. It is the oldest stone bridge of continuous spans existing in Beijing. The bridge is 266.5m long and about 7.5m wide in most sections with the widest area reaching 9.3m. There are

- 卢沟桥的狮子

1962年，有关部门曾对卢沟桥的狮子进行了清点，逐个编号登记，清点出大小石狮子共485个，至此应该说是"谜团冰释"了。不料在1979年的复查中，又发现了17个，这样大小石狮子的总数变为502个。

Stone Lions on the Lugou Bridge

In 1962 a government agency made an inventory of the stone lions on the Lugou Bridge and came up with a total of 485, which seemed to resolve the puzzle for the exact number of lions. But in 1979 when the inventory was rechecked, additional 17 stone lions were discovered. So the total number of big and small stone lions changed to 502.

卢沟桥始建于金大定二十九年（1189年），明正统九年（1444年）重修，清康熙年间毁于洪水，康熙三十七年（1698年）重建。早在战国时代，永定河一带已是交通要冲、兵家必争之地。原来只有浮桥相连，金朝定都燕京之后，原有的浮桥已不能适应都城的需要，于是被改建为石桥。

卢沟桥上的石刻十分精美，桥身的石雕护栏上共有望柱281根，柱高1.4米，柱头刻有莲花座，座下为荷叶墩，柱顶刻有众多的石狮，

10 bridge piers and 11 arches. It is a stone structure with key sections connected by iron pillars.

The Lugou Bridge was initially constructed in 1189 during the Jin Dynasty, rebuilt in 1444 during the Ming Dynasty, destroyed by flooding and rebuilt again in 1698 during the Qing Dynasty. As early as in the Warring States Period (475 B.C.-221 B.C.), the Yongding River area was considered a key transportation hub and fought for by different military rivals. Originally there was only one floating bridge. When Beijing became the capital of the Jin Dynasty (1115-1234), it was

● 卢沟桥全貌（图片提供：全景正片）
A Full View of the Lugou Bridge

神态各异。这些狮子有雌雄之分，雌的戏小狮，雄的弄绣球，有的大狮子身上还刻有几只小狮，最小的只有几厘米长，有的只露半个头、一张嘴，因此民间有句歇后语说："卢沟桥的石狮子——数不清。"

rebuilt into a stone bridge to meet the needs of the big city.

The exquisitely carved stone railings of the bridge are supported by 281 1.4m-high posts. Each post is carved with a lotus flower seat at the top surrounded by lotus leaves. Sitting on the lotus flower seats are stone lions of different postures and looks. There are male lions playing with embroidered balls and female lions playing with smaller lions. Some of the bigger lions even have baby lions carved on their body. The smallest lion is only a few centimeters long with half of its head and a mouth revealed. There is a folk saying, "Stone lions on Lugou Bridge are countless."

● "卢沟晓月"碑亭

古时候，每当黎明斜月西沉之时，明月倒映水中，更显明媚皎洁，所以"卢沟晓月"从金章宗年间就被列为"燕京八景"之一。1698年重修时，康熙帝下令在桥西头立碑，记述重修卢沟桥的事。桥东头则立有乾隆帝亲笔题写的"卢沟晓月"碑。

Stele Inscribed with "Morning Moon over Lugou Bridge"

In ancient times the scenery of Lugou Bridge was said to be more beautiful at dawn when the moon was about to set in the west and its reflection could still be seen in the water. Therefore the scenic beauty of "Morning Moon over Lugou Bridge" was regarded as one of the eight best attractions in Beijing during the Jin Dynasty(1115-1234). When it was reconstructed in 1698, Emperor Kangxi of Qing ordered to build a stele at the western end of the bridge to document the reconstruction. At the eastern end of the bridge stands the stele of "Morning Moon over Lugou Bride" inscribed by Emperor Qianlong.

卢沟桥事变

卢沟桥事变又称"七七事变"。1931年，日本侵吞中国东北后，为进一步挑起全面侵华战争，陆续运兵入关。到1936年，日军已从东、西、北三面包围了北平（今北京市）。1937年7月7日夜，卢沟桥的日本驻军径自在中国驻军阵地附近举行所谓的军事演习，并称有一名日军士兵失踪，要求进入北平西南的宛平县城（今卢沟桥街道）搜查，遭到中国守军的拒绝。日军随即进攻宛平城和卢沟桥，开枪开炮猛轰卢沟桥，向城内的中国守军进攻。中国守军第29军37师219团奋起还击，由此掀开了中华民族抗日战争的序幕。

Lugou Bridge Incident

The Lugou Bridge Incident is also known as the July 7th Incident. After its invasion of Northeast China in 1931, the Japanese army started to maneuver towards Central China for a full-scale war of aggression against China. By 1936, the Japanese army had surrounded the city of Beiping (today's Beijing) from the east, west and north. On the night of July 7th, 1937, the Japanese troops stationed around the Lugou Bridge carried out military training maneuvers without any advanced notice and claimed that one soldier was missing. They demanded to enter Wanping County (current Lugouqiao Street) to search for the missing solider and were rejected by the Chinese troops stationed in that area. Then the Japanese troops opened fire with machine guns and artilleries attacking the Chinese army stationed around the bridge. The Chinese army (219th Regiment, 37th Division, 29th Route Army) fought back heroically, which officially marked the beginning of the the Chinese People's War of Resistance Against Japanese Aggression.

- 宛平县城城墙

卢沟桥的东头是宛平县城，这是一座拱卫京都的小城，建于明末。1937年7月7日在这里爆发的"卢沟桥事变"，点燃了抗日战争的熊熊烈火，城墙上至今还留有累累弹痕。

City Walls in Wanping County

Wanping was a small city east of the Lugou Bridge built at the end of the Ming Dynasty to protect Beijing. The July 7th Incident of 1937 taking place here marked the beginning of the Chinese People's War of Resistance Against Japanese Aggression. Even today bullet holes from the incident can be seen on the city walls.

> 永通桥

永通桥坐落在北京通州区境内古老的通惠河上。通惠河是元代由水利学家郭守敬主持开凿的一条人

> Yongtong Bridge

The Yongtong Bridge sits across the ancient Tonghui River in Tongzhou District, Beijing. Tonghui River was a man-made watercourse designed by the

• 永通桥上的镇兽
Stone Carved Beasts on Yongtong Bridge

• 北京通州永通桥
Yongtong Bridge in Tongzhou District, Beijing

工河道，开通后成为京师联结东北和南方的咽喉要道，每年有大量的粮食和货物从京杭大运河经通惠河运到京城。永通桥的前身是一座木桥，因通惠河坡度较大，水流湍急，大雨季节河水暴涨，常将木桥冲毁，明代正统十一年（1446年）改建为石桥。

永通桥是一座三孔的券形石拱桥，南北长50米，宽16米。其与众不同之处是中间的桥洞特别高，可

hydrologist Guo Shoujing in the Yuan Dynasty. After its opening, Tonghui River became a key thoroughfare between Beijing and North/South China. Every year large amounts of grains and goods were transported to Beijing on the Beijing-Hangzhou Grand Canal via the Tonghui River. Originally Yongtong Bridge was a timber bridge often damaged or destroyed by surging water during the raining season due to the relatively steep river bed of the Tonghui

达8.5米，宽6.7米，而左右两孔仅高3.5米，相差悬殊。这是专为漕运的需要设计的。因为通惠河上的运粮船多为帆船，为避免阻碍漕船的航行，工匠将桥的中孔建造得相当高耸，漕船可直出直入，有所谓"八里桥不落桅"之说。

River. It was rebuilt into a stone bridge in 1446 during the Ming Dynasty.

The Yongtong Bridge is a stone bridge with three semicircular arches, 50m long from south to north and 16m wide. The distinctive feature of the bridge is its 8.5m high and 6.7m wide arch in the middle, significantly taller than the arch on each side with a height of only 3.5m. This was designed specifically to allow enough clearance for ships for grain transportation. Most of these ships were junk ships with high masts. There was a saying that ships for grain transportation could sail through Yongtong Bridge without lowering their masts.

京杭大运河

京杭大运河是中国乃至世界上最长的人工运河，北起北京（古称涿郡），南到杭州（古称余杭），经北京、天津两市及河北、山东、江苏、浙江四省，贯通海河、黄河、淮河、长江、钱塘江五大水系，全长1794公里。大运河的开凿最早始自春秋时期，吴王夫差开凿从江都（今扬州市）邗口至山阳（今淮安市）淮安末口的邗沟。到隋代，隋炀帝为了加强中央集权和南粮北运，自大业元年（605年）起下令开凿了京淮段至长江以南的运河。到元朝时，为了把粮食从南方运到北方，又先后开凿了三段河道，把原来以洛阳为中心的隋代运河，修筑成以都城大都（今北京）为中心，南下直达杭州的纵向运河。京杭运河对中国南北地区之间的经济、文化发展与交流，特别是对沿线地区工农业经济的发展和城镇的兴起均起了巨大作用。

Beijing-Hangzhou Grand Canal

The Beijing-Hangzhou Grand Canal is the longest man-made canal in China and in the world. Starting at Beijing in the north and ending in Hangzhou in the south, it is 1,794 kilometers long passing through Beijing, Tianjin and the provinces of Hebei, Shandong, Jiangsu and Zhejiang, and connecting to five big watercourses of Haihe River, the Yellow River, Huaihe River, the Yangtze River and Qiantang River. In the Spring and Autumn Period (770 B.C.–476 B.C.), King Fuchai of the State Wu started the construction from Jiangdu (present-day Yangzhou City) to Shanyang (present-day Huai'an City). Emperor Yang of the Sui Dynasty (581-618) ordered to build the section from Beijing and Huaihe River to the south of the Yangtze River in order to centralize the imperial power and facilitate grain transportation from the south to the north. Beginning from the year 605, three sections of the canal were completed changing the original watercourse around Luoyang City to a vertical canal starting from Beijing to Hangzhou in the south. The Beijing-Hangzhou Grand Canal has played a tremendous role in the economic growth, cultural development and exchanges between North and South China, particularly in the industrial, agricultural and economic development and the rise of cities and towns in the areas along the canal.

- 京杭大运河
Beijing-Hangzhou Grand Canal

> 赵州桥

赵州桥坐落在河北省赵县的洨河上，又名"安济桥"，建于隋大业年间，由著名匠师李春设计和建造，距今已有约1400年的历史，是中国现存最早、保存最完善的古代敞肩石拱桥。赵州桥长64.40米，跨度37.02米，拱圈矢高7.23米，两端宽9.6米，中间略窄，宽9米。因桥两端肩部各有两个小孔，故称"敞肩型"，这是世界造桥史上的一个创造。这种大拱加小拱的敞肩拱首先可以增加桥梁

- 李春雕像
  Statue of Li Chun

> Zhaozhou Bridge

The Zhaozhou Bridge, also known as the Anji Bridge, is situated on the Xiaohe River in Zhaoxian County, Hebei Province. Built between 605 and 618, it was designed and constructed by Li Chun, a famous craftsman in the Sui Dynasty. With a history of 1,400 years, it is the oldest open-spandrel stone arch bridge best preserved in China today. The Zhaozhou Bridge has a total length of 64.40m, a span of 37.02m and a 7.23m high arch. The bridge deck narrows in the middle with a 9m width and widens to 9.6m at both ends. The bridge has four smaller arches on the left and right exterior curve of the main arch. Known as the open-spandrel structure and considered an innovation in the world's bridge building history, this type of bridge structure, first of all, allows water to pass through when the bridge is

洨河上的赵州桥（图片提供：全景正片）
Zhaozhou Bridge on the Xiaohe River

● 赵州桥栏板上的石雕（图片提供：FOTOE）
Stone Carvings on the Railing Panels of the Zhaozhou Bridge

的泄洪能力，减轻洪水对桥的冲击力，提高大桥的安全性；其次，敞肩的设计可节省大量土石材料，减轻桥身的重量，从而增加桥梁的稳固性；而且大拱弧线优美，四个小拱均衡对称，使石桥显得更加轻巧秀丽。

submerged in a flood, thereby reducing the force on the structure from the floodwater and increasing the safety of the bridge. Secondly, the open-spandrel design saves lots of building materials and reduces the total weight of the bridge, which greatly improves the stability of the bridge. Thirdly it gives the bridge a light and elegant profile with a beautiful curved line of the big arch complemented by four symmetrical smaller arches.

> 桥楼殿

河北省井陉县境内的苍岩山，自古就以"雄、奇、秀、险、幽"闻名天下。始建于隋代的古寺福庆寺就依山就势位于苍岩山北侧的悬崖峭壁上。

作为福庆寺的主要建筑之一，桥楼殿是由桥和建在桥上的楼殿两部分组成，以桥作为承重结构。这座桥的形制与赵州桥极为相似，为单孔敞肩圆弧石拱桥，桥长15米，跨径10.7米，宽9米。桥拱脚处比拱顶处宽0.4米，以增强拱的稳定性。桥拱上镌刻着怪兽、骏马和人物，栩栩如生。桥横跨于对峙的断崖之间，距山涧底部约70米。桥上的桥楼殿为两层，面宽五间，进深三间，为重檐楼阁式建筑，坐西朝东，瓦顶平缓，飞檐翘角，具有清

> Bridge-Tower Hall
(Qiaolou Dian)

Situated in Jingxing County, Hebei Province, Cangyan Mountain is famous for its magnificence, peculiarity, elegance, precipitousness and seclusion. Buildings in the ancient Temple of Forture and Celebration (*Fuqing Si*) built in the Sui Dynasty (581-618) scatter on the precipices along the northern side of Cangyan Mountain.

As the central landmark in the temple, the Bridge-Tower Hall consists of a bridge serving as the load-bearing structure and a hall on the bridge. The bridge is an open-spandrel single-arch stone bridge structurally similar to the Zhaozhou Bridge. It is 15m long and 9m wide with a 10.7m span. The foot of the arch is 0.4m wider than the top of arch to increase the stability of the arch. The arch is carved with images of lifelike beasts, horses and

代早期建筑的特点。从桥下仰望，桥楼拱跨，犹如彩虹高挂，有与蓝天白云齐飞之感；而站在殿前凭栏俯瞰，沟底树木葱郁，远处重山叠嶂，更显桥楼的险峻。

human figures. The bridge spans across two confronting cliffs, about 70m from the bottom of the gorge below. The hall on the bridge is a two-story pavilion-style building with double eaves, five-room wide and three-room deep. Facing east, the hall has all the characteristics of the early Qing Dynasty architecture with a flat tile roof, upturned eaves and raised roof corners. Looking up from below the bridge, the arch resembles a rainbow hanging high in the sky with clouds. Looking down by the front railings of the hall, the lush greens at the bottom of the gorge and layers of mountain ridges in the distance make the Bridge-Tower Hall even more precipitous.

● 井陉桥楼殿（图片提供：FOTOE）
Bridge-Tower Hall in Jingxing County

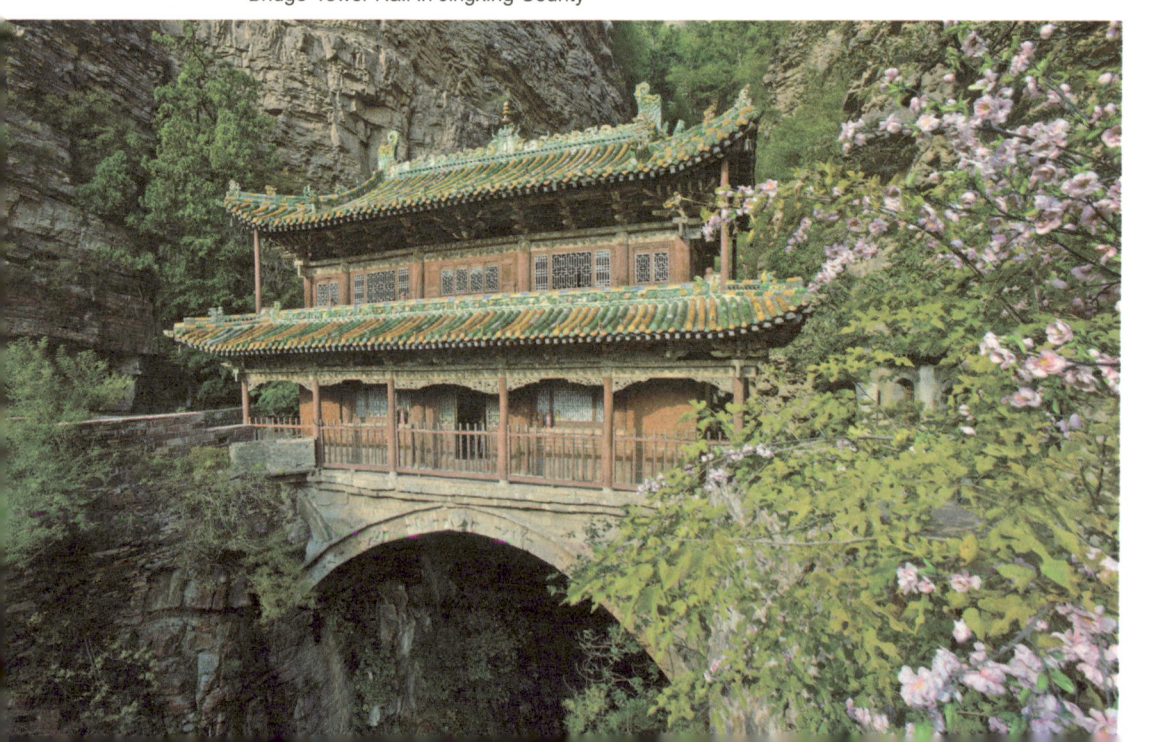

> 七孔桥

七孔桥，俗称"五音桥"，位于河北遵化的清东陵区内。清东陵是清朝两处帝后陵区中较大的一处。在这个陵区中，有顺治帝的孝陵、康熙帝的景陵、乾隆帝的裕陵、咸丰帝的定陵、同治帝的惠陵以及慈禧太后的定东陵等。其中，孝陵是清东陵中建筑最早、规模最大的一座陵墓，同时也是

> Seven-Arch Bridge (Qikong Qiao)

The Seven-Arch Bridge, also known as Five-Tone Bridge (*Wuyin Qiao*) is situated inside of the Eastern Imperial Mausoleums of the Qing Dynasty. The Eastern Imperial Mausoleums are the larger one in size between the two Qing-dynasty mausoleum complexes, which includs Xiaoling Mausoleum for Emperor Shunzhi, Jingling Mausoleum for

- 清东陵神道
  Sacred Way of the Eastern Imperial Mausoleums of the Qing Dynasty

清东陵陵区中的主体建筑。它正对着一条用砖石铺砌的神道，而七孔桥就处在从门口进入陵区的神道之上。

七孔桥与孝陵同时修建，是清东陵一百多座桥梁中的佼佼者。其桥长110米，宽9.08米。桥面两侧修有石栏杆，每侧各有望柱62根，桥下有拱券7个。全桥形态优美，肃穆壮观。

七孔桥的特殊之处在于它的桥栏板是用特殊石材制成的。据分

• 清东陵七孔桥 (图片提供：FOTOE)
Seven-Arch Bridge of the Eastern Imperial Mausoleums of the Qing Dynasty

Emperor Kangxi, Yuling Mausoleum for Emperor Qianlong, Dingling Mausoleum for Emperor Xianfeng, Huiling Mausoleum for Emperor Tongzhi and East Dingling Mausoleun for Empress Dowager Cixi. Xiaoling Mausoleum is the oldest and largest of all tombs in the Eastern Imperial Mausoleums of the Qing Dynasty. As the main building structure in the complex, the Xiaoling Mausoleum complex faces the brick-paved Sacred Way while the Seven-Arch Bridge stands on the Sacred Way leading to the entrance of the mausoleum.

The Seven-Arch Bridge was built at the same time as the Xiaoling Mausoleum and considered one of the best among over one hundred bridges in the Eastern Imperial Mausoleums of the Qing

析，七孔桥的栏板石中含有50%的方解石。这种石料含有铁质，因此在建桥的时候，工匠们根据每块栏板石含铁质的多少，按照中国古代"五音"宫、商、角、徵、羽的顺序，分别将它们安置在桥栏上。这样，当人们在桥上用手敲击栏板时，便会听到清脆悦耳的声音，"五音桥"之名因此而来。

Dynasty. It is 110m long and 9.08m wide with seven arches. The stone railings on each side of the bridge are supported by 62 posts. The bridge's profile is of elegance and solemnness.

The Seven-Arch Bridge is unique in its railing panels made of a special kind of stone material, which has 50% of calcites, according to some analysis. Depending on how much iron a specific stone slab contained, the bridge craftsmen installed each panel according to the sequence of the ancient Chinese five tones: *Gong* (Do), *Shang* (Re), *Jue* (Mi), *Zhi* (Sol) and *Yu* (La). It is called the Five-Tone Bridge after a peculiar acoustical phenomenon: by tapping gently on the railing panels, the five tones of the pentatonic scale can be heard.

> 小商桥

小商桥位于河南漯河临颍县与郾城区交界的小商河上，是一座红色石拱桥。据记载，此桥建于隋开皇四年（584年），比大名鼎鼎的河北赵州桥还早二三十年。小商桥全长21米，桥面宽7米，有三个桥洞，中间的桥洞大，两侧的较小。在中间桥孔的桥基上，以浮雕的手法雕刻着四个金刚力士像，形态威猛。中孔桥洞的拱券上，雕刻着龙、虎、狮子和天马等动物形象及莲花等图案，十分生动。在主拱和两侧小拱的交接处又各雕有一个龙头，伸向两侧河面。这些石雕使小商桥在浑厚朴实之中带有玲珑秀丽的风格。

> Xiaoshang Bridge

The Xiaoshang Bridge is a red stone arch bridge sitting across the Xiaoshang River along the common borders between Linying County and Yancheng City, Henan Province. According to historical records, this bridge was built in the year 584, over two or three decades earlier than the famous Zhaozhou Bridge in Hebei Province. The bridge is 21m long and 7m wide with one big arch in the middle and two smaller side arches. The mighty images of four Deva Kings are embossed on the center bridge pile. The middle arch crown is engraved with lively images of loongs, tigers, lions, mythical horses and lotus flowers. Between the main arch and the smaller side arch, there is a carved loong head protruding out to the riverbank. These stone carvings add a level of elegance to the earthy and simple Xiaoshang Bridge.

- 小商桥（图片提供：FOTOE）
Xiaoshang Bridge

小商桥与杨再兴

　　小商桥之所以有名，在于这里曾经发生过一起重大的历史事件。南宋时期，金兵南下，宋将岳飞率军抵抗。岳飞手下的大将杨再兴率领岳家军和金兵在小商桥一带展开大战。当时，他率领的岳家军只有三百余骑，而金兵却有十二万人。杨再兴不畏强敌，率兵斩杀金兵两千余人后，在小商河中被乱箭射死。他的事迹在《宋史•杨再兴传》中也有记载。从此，小商桥也随之名闻天下。而在小商桥东面不远处还有杨再兴墓，前往参观凭吊的人至今络绎不绝。

A Story of Xiaoshang Bridge and Yang Zaixing

The Xiaoshang Bridge is also well known for an important historical event. During the Southern Song Dynasty (1127-1279), General Yue Fei led his army to resist the invaders of the Jin Dynasty. His lieutenant Yang Zaixing and his troop fought a big battle in the area around the Xiaoshang Bridge. With his 300 cavalrymen against over 120,000 Jin-dynasty solders, Yang was finally shot to death by arrows from the Jin-dynasty army. This event was documented in his biography in *The History of Song Dynasty*. After that, the Xiaoshang Bridge became famous in China. Even today, many visitors go to pay respect at Yang Zaixing's memorial built not far from the bridge.

> 永安石桥

永安石桥又名"大石桥",在辽宁沈阳的西郊,横跨在蒲河的河面上。据记载,永安石桥建于清太宗崇德六年(1641),是由石匠任朝贵主持修建的。在永安桥的东头立有一块石碑,正面刻着"宽温仁圣皇帝敕建永安桥"的碑文,石碑的背面还刻写着催工、督工等官员的姓名,以及"石匠任朝贵"等字样。

永安桥是一座三孔石拱桥。桥长37米,桥面宽14.5米,每个拱券的跨度均为13米。在永安桥桥面的左右两侧,分别立有石雕望柱19根,柱间安置着石栏板。望柱的顶端雕刻着许多神态各异的石狮子。位于桥面两端的望柱制作成石鼓形,鼓面上雕刻着飞鸟、走兽和花卉等

> Yong'an Stone Bridge

The Yong'an Stone Bridge, also known as "The Big Stone Bridge" stands across Pu River in the western suburbs of Shenyang City, Liaoning Province. According to historical records, it was built in 1641 during the reign of Emperor Taizong of the Qing Dynasty under the supervision of stonemason Ren Chaogui. At the east end of the bridge is a stone stele with a front inscription of "Yong'an Bridge Built by the Order of the Benevolent Emperor" and a back inscription listing the names of foremen and supervisors as well as the stonemason Ren Chaogui.

The Yong'an Bridge is a three-arch stone bridge, 37m long and 14.5m wide with a 13m span for each arch. Each side of the bridge has 19 stone-carved railing posts with stone panels in between. There are stone lions in different postures carved at the top of each post. The drum-shaped

• 沈阳永安石桥（图片提供：CFP）
Yong'an Stone Bridge in Shenyang City

图案，石栏板上的花纹为柿蒂的形状。这些都为雄伟的石桥增加了秀丽的色彩。此桥最为特殊之处是在石桥中拱的南侧，伸出两条龙，龙头在北，龙尾在南，构成了一组二龙托桥的形象，尤其是水位上升与龙体持平时，效果特别明显。

posts at the two bridge ends have images of birds, animals and flowers engraved on top. The railing panels are carved in the pattern of persimmon's pedicle. All these stone carvings and sculptures make this magnificent stone bridge more enchanting. The most spectacular feature of this bridge must be the two loong sculptures on the middle arch in the south side of bridge with the two loong heads visible from the north and two loong tails visible from the south as if the bridge was supported by two loongs. This effect is more apparent when the water level reaches to the two loong bodies.

> 鱼沼飞梁

鱼沼飞梁位于山西太原的晋祠之内，处于献殿和圣母殿之间。桥的平面呈十字形，造型和结构都非常特殊。北魏水利学家郦道元（约470—527）在公元6世纪所著的《水经注·晋水》中，就已经有了鱼沼飞梁的记载，可见，鱼沼飞梁的初建当在北魏之前。

"鱼沼"就是鱼池，"飞梁"就是桥梁，"鱼沼飞梁"既是桥梁的名称，又是对这座桥位置和形态的一个生动概括。鱼沼指的是太原晋祠圣母殿

- 鱼沼飞梁旁的石兽
The Stone Animal beside the Flying Bridge aross the Fish Pond

> Flying Bridge across the Fish Pond (Yuzhao Feiliang)

The Flying Bridge across the Fish Pond is situated between the Offerings Hall (*Xian Dian*) and the Saint Mother's Hall (*Shengmu Dian*) inside the Jinci Temple in Taiyuan City, Shanxi Province. The structure and style are unusual in its cross-shaped layout. A hydrologist Li Daoyuan(about 470-527) of the Northern Wei Dynasty (386-534) documented this bridge in his book about rivers in Shanxi Province. His writing proves that the bridge had been built before the Northern Wei Dynasty.

Yuzhao means a fish pond and *Feiliang* means bridge beams. The Flying Bridge across the Fish Pond is not only the name of the bridge, but also a vivid summary of the bridge's position and its shape. The fish pond refers to the square-shaped pond in front of the Saint

● 太原晋祠鱼沼飞梁
The Flying Bridge across Fish Pond in Jinci Temple, Taiyuan City

前的方形水池。水池上立有38根小八角形石柱，柱顶架斗拱和枕梁，承托着十字形桥面。东西桥面长15.5米，宽5米，高出地面13米，东西向连接圣母殿与献殿。南北桥面长

Mother's Hall in the temple. Over the pond there are 38 small octagonal stone columns supporting the arches, beams and the cross-shaped deck of the bridge. The bridge deck from east to west is 15.5m long, 5m wide and 13m above the

18.8米，宽33米，两端下斜至岸边，整个造型犹如展翅欲飞的大鸟，故称"飞梁"。飞梁正桥和翼桥的两侧，都安装了汉白玉石栏杆，在正桥东头的望柱上，北侧刻有"鱼沼"二字，南侧刻有"飞梁"二字。

鱼沼飞梁究竟初建于何时，何朝何代进行过怎样的修缮，史书上都没有记载。

ground connected with the Saint Mother's Hall to the east and the Offerings Hall to the west. The deck from south to north is 18.8m long and 33m wide gradually sloping down to the edge of the pond on each of the four sides. The entire structure looks like a big bird about to fly by flapping the wings, hence the Flying Bridge. The center of the bridge and the four side sections all have white-marble railings. At the east end of the bridge, characters *Yu* and *Zhao* were carved on the railing post in the north side and characters *Fei* and *Liang* were carved on the post in the south side of the bridge.

No historical records have been found about the time of the bridge's initial construction and the dynasties of its repairs and rebuilding.

太原晋祠

晋祠位于山西太原西南郊25公里处的悬瓮山下，祠内有几十座古建筑，山环水绕，古木参天，泉水蜿蜒穿流于祠庙殿宇之间，环境幽雅，风景秀丽。

晋祠内建筑布局由中、北、南三部分组成。中部建筑结构壮丽而整肃，为全祠的核心；北部建筑以崇楼高阁取胜；南部建筑楼阁林立，小桥流水，亭榭环绕。整个建筑群布局紧凑、严密，既像庙观院落，又好似皇室的宫苑。

宏伟壮丽的圣母殿位于晋祠建筑布局中轴线的末端，创建于北宋天圣年间，是晋祠内现存最古老的建筑。圣母殿内有43尊泥塑彩绘人像，多为北宋时期原塑，造型生动,姿态自然。晋祠内的圣母殿彩塑、相传植于西周的周柏、长流不息的难老泉被合称为"晋祠三绝"。

Jinci Temple in Taiyuan City

The Jinci Temple is located in the Xuanweng Mountain ranging 25 kilometers southwest of Taiyuan, Shanxi Province. In the temple there are dozens of ancient building structures surrounded by mountains and ancient pine trees with spring waterways flowing between ancient halls. The temple enjoys a quiet and secluded environment with beautiful scenery.

The building structures are clustered in the center, the north and the south of the complex. The entire layout is well organized with magnificent and solemn centrad structures, tall buildings in the north and many pavilions around small bridges and creeks in the south. The whole complex looks like a temple and an imperial garden.

Situated at the end of the central axis in the Jinci Temple, the glorious Saint Mother's Hall is the oldest extant ancient building in the complex, built during the Northern Song Dynasty (960-1279). Inside the hall stand 43 painted clay figures, most of which are originals from the Song Dynasty. The acclaimed three wonders in the Jinci Temple are the painted clay sculptures in the Saint Mother's Hall, the Cypress said to be planted in the Western Zhou Dynasty (1046 B.C.-771 B.C.) and the endless stream of the Never Aging Spring (*Nanlao Quan*).

• 晋祠圣母殿中的泥塑圣母像
Clay Sculpture of Saint Mother in the Saint Mother's Hall of Jinci Temple

• 晋祠难老泉亭
The Never Aging Spring Pavilion in Jinci Temple

> 放生桥

　　放生桥在上海青浦朱家角镇的东面，横跨于漕港之上，是一座古代的联拱石桥。放生桥地处青浦县和昆山县之间，过去两县之间因为无桥，交通往来仅靠船渡，十分不

> Fangsheng Bridge

The Fangsheng Bridge (meaning setting fish free bridge) is situated across the Caogang River east of Zhujiajiao Town, Qingpu District, Shanghai. It is an ancient stone bridge of continuous spans. In the old days there was no bridge

便。明隆庆五年（1571年），附近的慈门寺僧人募款造桥，并规定在桥下一定范围内只能放生鱼鳖，不能撒网捕鱼，故名"放生桥"。明清时代，每月农历初一，当地僧人都要在桥上举行放生仪式，将活鱼放入河中。

放生桥长达70.8米，桥面宽5.8米。全桥共五孔，中孔最高最大，左右两侧各两孔。桥的设计采用了超薄的桥墩，加上桥拱自然递增，

between Qingpu and Kunshan counties and transportation depended only on inconvenient ferryboats. In 1571, monks in nearby Cimen Temple raised funds to build a bridge. They also stated that fish-catching was not allowed under the bridge and people could only set fish free in areas around the bridge, hence the name "Setting Fish Free (*Fangsheng*) Bridge". During the Ming and Qing dynasties every year on the first day of the lunar calendar, the monks would hold

• 上海朱家角放生桥（图片提供：FOTOE）
Fangsheng Bridge in Zhujiajiao Town, Shanghai

全桥形成一个缓和的纵坡，自然衔接两岸街面，显得雄伟而不笨重。桥上的石刻也很精细，龙门石上雕有8条蟠龙，桥顶四角蹲着4只石狮，仰头张嘴，栩栩如生。桥面中央镶嵌有雕花石板。桥东建有碑亭，供行人休憩；临水筑石驳，为船楫停泊所用。放生桥长如带、形如虹，朱家角十景之一的"井带长虹"指的就是此桥。

a ceremony on the bridge to release live fish into the water.

The Fangsheng Bridge is 70.8m long and 5.8m wide on the deck with five arches, two arches on each side of the larger and higher middle arch. It was designed to use extremely slender bridge piers to support the continuous spans to form a gentle slope naturally extending to the roads on both riverbanks. The bridge is magnificent, but not heavy. The exquisite stone carvings on the bridge include eight coiling loongs on the arches and four mouth-opened, vivid stone lions on the top of the middle railing panels. A stone slab engraved with flower patterns is mounted in the center of the bridge deck. The stele pavilion at the east end of the bridge provides a rest place for pedestrians. A dock near the bridge serves as a landing area for boats. The bridge is one of the ten best sights in Zhujiajiao for its rainbow shape and resemblance of a long belt.

- **朱家角河上的乌篷船**

朱家角又称"角里"，早在宋元时期已形成集市，因水运方便，商业日渐繁盛，至明万历年间已经成为繁荣的大镇。作为水乡古镇，朱家角水多、桥多，河埠多，造型各异的石桥遍布全镇的大河小巷。

Covered Boats in Zhujiajiao River

Zhujiajiao Town, also known as Jiaoli, became a market place as early as in the Song and Yuan dynasties. Thanks to the easy transportation in the surrounding waterways, trades flourished and the small village grew into a bigger and prosperous town. Besides, this town is well-known for its abundant water resources, rivers and docks with stone bridges of different shapes and styles scattered everywhere in the town.

> 云间第一桥

云间第一桥位于上海松江西侧，南北横跨于古浦塘上，又名"跨塘桥"。据记载，云间第一桥初建于南宋，那时还是一座木桥。

> Yunjian No. 1 Bridge

The Yunjian No. 1 Bridge is situated to the west of Songjiang District, Shanghai across Gupu Pond from south to north, also known as Kuatang Bridge (meaning crossing the pond bridge). According to

- 上海松江云间第一桥
  Yunjian No. 1 Bridge in Songjiang District, Shanghai

在明代某年端午节的一次龙舟竞赛上，观众挤于桥上，桥因超重而坍塌。明成化年间，知府王衡在旧址上重建石桥，由于松江地区古称"云间"，此桥又是当时松江最大的一座桥，所以改名为"云间第一桥"。全桥共3孔，长49.3米，高8米。桥面两侧安有护栏。在桥东侧的护栏石下，刻着"云间第一桥"五个大字。此桥的桥顶和桥薄墩十分纤秀，保留着端庄雄伟、古朴典雅的风貌，体现出江南古桥的特色。

historical records, it was first built as a timber bridge in the Southern Song Dynasty (1127-1279). During a Loong Boat Festival in the Ming Dynasty (1368-1644), the bridge collapsed from being overloaded with crowded onlookers for the loong boat racing. A stone bridge was built by a local government official Wang Heng at the same location between 1465 and 1487. In the past, the Songjiang area was called "Yunjian", so the bridge's name was changed to "No. 1 Bridge in Yunjian", also because it was the largest bridge in Songjiang at the time. The bridge is 49.3m long and 8m high with three arches and railings on both sides of the deck. The bridge's name in five big Chinese characters was carved below a stone rail on the east side. This bridge retains a simple and elegant style with delicately built bridge deck and slender piers demonstrating the characteristics of the ancient bridges south of the Yangtze River.

> 金莲桥

　　金莲桥位于江苏无锡惠山寺的御碑亭前，建于宋代，由宋代名相李纲主持修建，距今已有800多年的历史。

　　金莲桥为三孔石梁桥，桥长10.7米，宽3.4米。中孔稍高，平面长，东西两边孔成楔形而稍短，桥身略成弧形。桥端为石砌桥台，石梁两端雕成神鱼首形。两座石砌桥墩的石梁上，雕有四个螭首。桥台与桥墩间，每孔组排六块石梁，中间四块为桥面石，以通行人；桥的两侧石栏板外侧雕刻着宋代典型的"压地隐起缠枝牡丹间化生（童子）"图案，极为典雅华美，寓意富贵吉祥。金莲桥整体造型优美、匀称、稳固，而且雕饰华美，为古代石桥中不多见的上佳之作。

> Golden Lotus Bridge (Jinlian Qiao)

The Golden Lotus Bridge is situated in front of the Imperial Stele Pavilion in the Huishan Temple of Wuxi City, Jiangsu Province. It was built over 800 years ago during the Song Dynasty (960-1279) under the supervision of Li Gang, a well-known general.

The Golden Lotus Bridge is a stone beam bridge with three openings, 10.7m long and 3.4m wide. The opening in the center is relatively higher with a flat and long top sided in the east and west by two wedge-shaped lower openings. The bridge is slightly arched. The stone beams supported by two stone abutments were carved with a celestial fish head at each end. Four ancient loong heads were engraved on the two stone piers. There are six stone beams for each of the opening, four of which are used as bridge

● 惠山寺御碑亭前的金莲桥 （图片提供：FOTOE）

金莲桥得名于桥下的金莲池，池内的千叶金莲原为南北朝时所种。唐代诗人曾有"千叶莲花旧有香，半山金刹照方塘"的诗句。

Golden Lotus Bridge in Front of the Imperial Stele Pavilion in the Huishan Temple

The Golden Lotus Bridge was named after the Golden Lotus Pond below the bridge. According to the legend, the golden lotus with a thousand leaves was planted during the Northern and Southern dynasties. A Tang-dynasty poet describes the scenery as "fragrance from the golden lotus with a thousand leaves and the golden temple in mid-hills shining on the square pond".

deck for pedestrians. The outer part of the railing panels were carved with typical Song-dynasty peony patterns, resplendent and elegant representing wealth and auspiciousness. The Golden Lotus Bridge is considered a rare masterpiece among ancient bridges for its beautiful, well-balanced and stable structure and gorgeous stone carvings.

> 七瓮桥

七瓮桥，又名"七桥瓮"，因桥下有7个半圆形的桥洞而得名，位于南京城南的光华门外，横跨于秦淮河上。七瓮桥始建于明代初期，原名为"上坊桥"，清代时重修，改名"七桥瓮"。在桥洞中孔的石券上，至今还保留着"清顺治六年（1649年）重修"的字样。

- 南京七瓮桥（图片提供：FOTOE）
Seven-Urn Bridge in Nanjing

> Seven-Urn Bridge (Qiweng Qiao)

The Seven-Urn Bridge, also known as "Seven Bridge-Urns" (*Qiqiao Weng*), got the name from its seven semicircular arches. It is located right outside of the Guanghua Gate of Nanjing city across the Qinhuai River. Built in the early Ming Dynasty, it was originally named "Shangfang Bridge". When it was rebuilt in the Qing Dynasty, the name was changed to "*Qiqiao Weng*". On the middle arch crown the inscriptions "Rebuilt in the 6th year of Reign of

七瓮桥长89.6米，桥面宽13米，高25米，桥下有6个桥墩、7个桥洞，中间的桥洞最大，跨径为10.4米。两侧的桥洞跨度逐渐变小，靠河岸的两个桥洞最小，跨度均为8.7米。桥墩为船形，迎水的一面向前突出达3米，上面刻有鳞甲斑斑的石兽，兽头凸起，不仅美观，而且具有标明水位的作用。在拱券的两侧均刻有螭首，现存螭首共有15个。七瓮桥在初建时全部用青石砌成，后来重修时部分改用了花岗石。石与石之间以石灰与糯米汁拌浆粘接，十分牢固。600多年来，七瓮桥一直在内河航运上发挥着重要作用。

Emperor Shunzhi of the Qing Dynasty" are still legible.

The bridge is 89.6m long and 25m high with a 13m wide bridge deck. There are 6 bridge piers and 7 arches, of which the middle arch is the largest with a span of 10.4m. The side arches become smaller gradually with the two smallest end arches having an 8.7m span. The boat-shaped bridge piers extend about 3 meters out on the side facing the water flow. Sculpted on the piers are head-protruding stone beasts covered with scales. They serve not only as a decoration, but also an instrument to display the water level. There are a total of 15 ancient loong heads, two on each side of an arch. The bridge was initially constructed all with bluestones. Granite slabs were used later in some places when it was rebuilt. The stone slabs were firmly joined together by a mixture of limestone powder and glutinous rice paste. Over the past 600 years, the bridge has played an important role in the inner river transportation.

风情万种的秦淮河

秦淮河是流经南京的第一大河，分内河和外河。流入城里的内秦淮河东西水关之间的河段，自三国时期的东吴以来就是繁华的商业区。六朝时，秦淮河畔成为名门望族的聚居之地，商贾汇集，文人会聚。隋唐以后，这里虽渐趋衰落，却吸引了无数文人骚客来此凭吊。到了宋代，十里秦淮逐渐复苏为江南文化中心。明清两代，尤其是明代，是十里秦淮的鼎盛时期，金粉楼台，鳞次栉比；画舫凌波，桨声灯影，构成一幅如梦如幻的美景。如今的秦淮河两岸全是古色古香的建筑群，飞檐漏窗，雕梁画栋，加之人文荟萃、市井繁华，集中体现了金陵古都的风貌，被称为"中国第一历史文化名河"。

Scenic and Charming Qinhuai River

Qinhuai River is the largest river flowing through the city of Nanjing. It is divided into inner and outer rivers. The inner Qinhuai River is the section between the watercourses coming from the east and the west. The inner river had been a bustling business district since the Three Kingdoms Period. By the Six dynasties, the Qinhuai riverbanks became populated by nobilities, rich merchants and scholars. After the Sui and Tang dynasties, the place gradually declined, but still attracted numerous poets and writers who came to pay their tribute. In the Song Dynasty, the ten-mile riverbanks along the inner Qinhuai River gradually revived into a cultural center south of the Yangtze River reaching its peak during the Ming and Qing dynasties. Particularly in the Ming Dynasty, this area presented a dream-like beauty of splendid pavilions and painted boats with red lanterns everywhere. Today the riverbanks on both sides of the Qinhuai River are filled with ancient-style building structures of double eaves, garden windows, carved beams, and painted pillars, which are perfectly blended into the history, culture and folk customs of the ancient city of Nanjing. The place is acclaimed as the "No. 1 River of History and Culture in China".

- 夜色中的秦淮河
  Night Scene of Qinhuai River

> 宝带桥

宝带桥又名"小长桥",位于江苏苏州葑门外长桥村,横跨在玳玳河上。

据史料记载,宝带桥建于唐代元和十一年至十四年(816—819),是由当时的苏州刺史王仲舒主持修建的。据说由于筑桥的经费欠缺,王仲舒将皇帝赏赐的一条金带都卖掉了。人们为了纪念王仲舒,便将这座石桥取名为"宝带桥"。之后的千余年间,宝带桥屡毁屡建,现存的石桥是按原貌修复的。

宝带桥是用花岗岩石砌筑而成的,桥长317米,桥面宽4.1米,桥下共有53孔。全桥构造复杂而结构轻盈,中间的三个桥洞特别高,可以通行大船,两旁各拱路面逐渐下

> Precious Belt Bridge (Baodai Qiao)

The Precious Belt Bridge, also known as the "Small Long Bridge (*Xiaochang Qiao*)", is located in the Changqiao Village outside of Fengmen Gate of Suzhou City, Jiangsu Province across the Daidai River.

According to historical records, its initial construction began between 816 and 819 during the Tang Dynasty under the supervision of Wang Zhongshu, a magistrate in Suzhou. It is said that Wang sold a gold belt bestowed to him by the emperor to finance the bridge construction due to the budget shortage. In memory of Wang, the bridge was named the "Precious Belt Bridge". The bridge was destroyed and rebuilt many times in the past thousand years The existing stone bridge was restored based on the original appearance.

降，形成弓形弧线。在桥的南北两端还各有石狮一对。桥北有一座高约3米的石塔，一座碑亭，亭内立有清代张松声撰写的石碑一块。在中国现今保存完整的古桥中，桥身如此之长、桥洞如此之多的古代石桥，宝带桥要算首屈一指的了。

- 苏州宝带桥（图片提供：FOTOE）
宝带桥改善了大运河和澹台湖之间的交通条件。其制造精巧，加上周围有青山绿水相衬，恰似飘动在水乡原野上的一条宝带，更显绮丽多姿。

Precious Belt Bridge in Suzhou
The Precious Belt Bridge not only has improved the transportation between the Grand Canal and Dantai Lake, but also has demonstrated its beautiful design resembling a precious belt floating in the water against a background of lush green mountains and rivers.

Built with granite stones, the Precious Belt Bridge has a length of 317m, a deck width of 4.1m and a total of 53 arches. The bridge structure is complex, but light. The three very tall center arches were designed to allow enough clearance for big vessels. The bridge deck above the side arches has a gradual slope. A couple of lion stone sculptures stand on each of the northern and southern ends. To the north of the bridge there are a 3-meter high stone pagoda and a stele pavilion with a stele inside inscribed by Zhang Songsheng of the Qing Dynasty. The Precious Belt Bridge is considered one of the best-preserved extant ancient bridges with a very long bridge deck and a great many arches.

> 枫桥

枫桥位于江苏省苏州市阊门外的枫桥镇，横跨于古运河的枫桥湾上。《苏州市志》上说，这里是古代的水陆交通要道，设护粮卡。每当漕粮北运经此，就封锁河道，

> Maple Bridge *(Feng Qiao)*

The Maple Bridge stands across the Maple Bridge Bay of the ancient Grand Canal outside of Changmen Gate, Suzhou City, Jiangsu Province. According to the ancient *Suzhou City Records,* this area used to be the intersection between water

• 苏州枫桥
Maple Bridge in Suzhou

• 寒山寺钟楼

寒山寺建于南朝梁代天监年间，原名"妙利普明塔院"。唐贞观年间，传说当时的名僧寒山和拾得曾来此住持，改名"寒山寺"。传说张继诗中的钟原来就悬于这里的钟楼上。现在钟楼里的大钟是清光绪三十二年（1906年）重铸的。

Bell Tower of the Hanshan Temple

The Hanshan Temple was built between the year 502 and 519 during the Southern dynasties and originally named "Miaoli Puming Temple". As the famous monk Hanshan and Shide lived here as abbots, the name was changed to "Hanshan Temple". It is said that the bell mentioned in Zhang Ji's poem was hung in the temple's bell tower. The current bell in the tower was recast in 1906 during the Qing Dynasty.

禁止别的船只通行，故名为"封桥"。枫桥是一座单孔石拱桥，全长38.7米，高7米，桥面宽3米，跨度为9.8米。桥的两端各有石阶20级，为人们上下桥提供了方便。

and land traffic where a checkpoint was set up for the safety of boats carrying grains. Whenever these boats passed by on their way to the north, the waterway would be blocked to stop other boats. Therefore it is called Feng Bridge meaning a blocking bridge. The Chinese characters for "maple" and "blocking" have the same pronunciation. The Maple Bridge is a single-arch stone bridge, 38.7m long, 7m tall and 3m wide with a span of 9.8m. There is a stairway of 20 steps on either side of the bridge for pedestrians.

Between the year 713 and 756 during the Tang Dynasty, poet Zhang Ji visited this area leaving behind a famous poem *"Night Mooring by the Maple Bridge"*, which reads, "While I watch the moon go down, a crow caws through the frost; by the Maple Bridge looking at the fishermen's torches here and there, I sit by myself and feel all alone; and I hear the midnight bell from the Hanshan Temple outside of Suzhou ringing in my boat." It is said that Zhang Ji wrote this poem on his way back to his hometown after he failed the Imperial Examination. His verses blended his depression with the late fall scenery showing brightness against darkness and silence against movement. The poem describes fully his

唐开元、天宝年间，大诗人张继经过此地时，曾留下名诗《枫桥夜泊》："月落乌啼霜满天，江枫渔火对愁眠。姑苏城外寒山寺，夜半钟声到客船。"据说这是张继赶考落第，郁郁回乡，途经此处写下的诗篇。诗中把旅途中的愁闷与周围深秋的景色融为一体，有明有暗，有静有动，描绘出悠远旷达的意境。这首诗令枫桥名闻天下。枫桥究竟始建于何时，现已无从确知。但是，古运河开凿于隋代，而张继是唐代中期（约8世纪）人，据此推断，枫桥当始建于唐代前期。在建成以后的一千多年间，枫桥曾数次毁坏，又多次重修。

mood and the artistic conception of the environment making the Maple Bridge well known in China. However, there is no historical record showing when the bridge was built. It can be inferred that the Maple Bridge was built in early Tang Dynasty based on the facts that the ancient Grand Canal was first constructed in the Sui Dynasty and Zhang Ji lived around mid-Tang Dynasty (approx. 8th century). Over a thousand years after it was built, the Maple Bridge went through many destructions and rebuilding.

• 年画《寒山寺》（清代）
Hanshan Temple, New Year Picture (Qing Dynasty, 1616-1911)

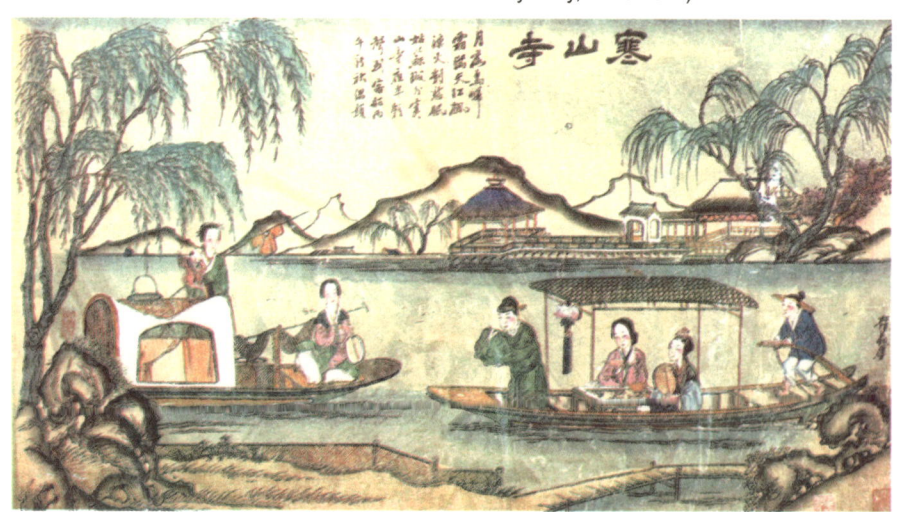

> 灭渡桥

灭渡桥位于苏州赤门湾，东西向横跨于古运河之上。

灭渡桥所在的赤门湾，正处于苏州市东面和南面两条外城河道的交汇处，也是大运河从苏州到杭州的咽喉地带，过往行人、车马和船只都非常多，是一个重要的交通枢纽。据记载，元朝元贞年间，此处设有渡船，客商、百姓在此过渡时屡屡遭到船家的敲诈勒索。昆山僧人敬修经过这里，因无钱而受到船家的刁难，于是发誓筹款建桥。他会同当地一些名士募集银钱，终于在元大德四年（1300年）三月建成此桥。人们便把它定名为"灭渡桥"。

灭渡桥是一座单孔石拱桥，全长78.5米，桥面宽4.5米，高9.5米，跨度为19.8米。桥的东西两端拓

> Miedu Bridge

The Miedu Bridge (meaning the bridge of getting rid of ferries) stands from east to west across the ancient Grand Canal in the Chimen Bay outside of Suzhou City.

The Chimen Bay is at the juncture of two watercourses, one from the east and one from the south of Suzhou City. This area used to be a major transportation intersection of the Grand Canal from Suzhou to Hangzhou with many pedestrians, carriages and boats. It was documented that between 1295 and 1296 during the Yuan Dynasty there were only ferry boats on the river. Merchants and other travelers were often cheated and overcharged by ferry owners. When a monk called Jing Xiu passed this area, he got very frustrated with the boat owners because he was bullied for having no money, so he was determined to raise funds to build a bridge. Together with

宽，大体上呈喇叭形。桥北筑有金刚墙，墙下有凸出墙外约1.5米、露出水面约1米的桥墩。这种桥墩和金刚墙可防止洪水与船只直接冲击桥体，对桥体起到保护作用。在桥体的南北两面，各有伸出的梁头三对，最上面的一对为青石雕兽头，下面的两对以花岗岩做成，没有任何装饰。桥的总体造型朴素大方，雄伟壮观。

苏州灭渡桥（图片提供：FOTOE）
Miedu Bridge of Suzhou

some notable local people, they were able to raise enough money and complete the construction of the bridge in March, 1300 during the Yuan Dynasty. And the bridge was named "Miedu" meaning to get rid of ferry boats.

The Miedu Bridge is a single-arch stone bridge with a total length of 78.5m, a deck width of 4.5m, a height of 9.5m and a span of 19.8m. It is shaped like a trumpet with two wider ends in the east and the west. To the north of the bridge hidden walls were built to reinforce bridge piers, which protrude 1.5m out from the walls and 1m above the water. The piers with the reinforced walls help to protect the bridge from being hit directly by flooding water or boats. In both the south and north ends of the bridge there are three pairs of protruding beams. The upper pair was carved with bluestone beast heads and the two lower pairs are just simple granite stones with no decorations. The bridge has a simple and magnificent appearance.

> 吴门桥

吴门桥位于江苏省苏州市西南隅的盘门外，横跨在古运河上，地处运河与大龙江的交汇处，是苏州市区通往太湖的必经之道。在吴门桥兴修之前，人们从苏州前往太湖等地，出城进城只能靠船渡，十分不便。北宋元丰七年（1084年），当地一位石姓富翁出资在这里修建了一座桥梁，人称"新桥"。新桥的北段是两座相连的木桥，南段是一座石桥，又被称为三条桥。后来人们拆除了新桥，重修了一座三孔石拱桥。

吴门桥全长66.3米，桥面宽5米，拱高9.5米，拱券跨径16米。桥洞正中刻有"吴门桥"三个大字。桥以苏州金山花岗岩构筑，杂有少量宋代旧桥所遗的武康石。在桥的

> Wumen Bridge

The Wumen Bridge is situated outside of the Panmen Gate at the southwest corner of Suzhou, Jiangsu Province across the ancient Grand Canal at the juncture between the Grand Canal and Dalong River. It is on the necessary route from Suzhou City to Taihu Lake. Before it was built, people had to rely on inconvenient ferryboats to travel from Suzhou City to Taihu Lake. In 1084 during the Northern Song Dynasty, a rich man whose family name is Shi financed the construction of the bridge, which was then called the "New Bridge". The northern part of the New Bridge consisted of two connected timber bridges and the southern part was a stone bridge. Therefore, the New Bridge was also known as the Three Strips Bridge. Later the New Bridge was demolished and a 3-arch stone bridge was rebuilt.

两端，分别用整块条石砌台阶50级。在桥北的金刚墙左边还有用石砌的纤道，宽约0.6米，为纤夫们拉船提供了方便。

The Wumen Bridge is 66.3m long, 5m wide on the deck and 9.5m high with a 16m span. The bridge's name is carved on the center arch crown in three big Chinese characters. The bridge was mainly built with granite stones from the Golden Mountain (*Jin Shan*) of Suzhou mixed with a small quantity of Wukang stones (a kind of tuff) from the old bridge site of the Song Dynasty. The bridge deck is paved with complete stone blocks, 50 steps on each side. On the left side of the hidden walls lies a stone towpath about 0.6m in width for the convenience of boat trackers.

• 苏州吴门桥
Wumen Bridge of Suzhou

- 苏州盘门水城门

过吴门桥不远就是盘门，是苏州现存最古的一座城门，也是中国现存陆城门和水城门并存的唯一一座城门。离此不远处，还耸立着北宋时期修建的瑞光塔。吴门桥建成后，和盘门、瑞光塔一起，构成了苏州市西南部著名的"盘门三景"。

Panmen Gate, a Gate Built above the Water, in Suzhou

The Panmen Gate not very far across the Wumen Bridge is the oldest extant city gate of Suzhou and the only gate existing today in China that combines both the gates in land and above water. The Ruiguang Pagoda of the Northern Song Dynasty stands not very far from the Panmen Gate. The Panmen Gate, the Ruiguang Pagoda and the Wumen Bridge became the famous "three attractions around the Panmen Gate" in the southwest of Suzhou.

> 大虹桥

大虹桥位于江苏扬州,初建于明朝末年。大虹桥最初是一座木桥,因两侧扶栏上涂以红漆,所以初名"红桥"。桥下有四层桥桩,每层均有四根木柱。全桥共有六层桥板,每层均有四块木板。桥面两侧围有木栏,全被漆为红色。清代乾隆元年(1736年),人们将木桥改建为单孔石拱桥,因远望去若垂虹饮涧,更名"虹桥"。乾隆十六年(1751年),人们还在桥上建了一座方亭。由于风雨侵蚀,方亭早已毁坏。

大虹桥面对瘦西湖的宽阔处,波光云影,水天一色。桥西的柳堤始修于隋代,清代时,人们在堤上种柳植花,每至春季,杨柳依依,鲜花盛开,这里被称为扬州北郊的

> Big Rainbow Bridge (Dahong Qiao)

The Big Rainbow Bridge in Yangzhou City, Jiangsu Province was originally a timber bridge built at the end of the Ming Dynasty. It was named "the Red Bridge" after the red painted railings. The original bridge had four-level bridge piers with four wooden columns on each level and a six-level bridge deck with four wooden boards on each level. The railings on the bridge were all painted red. In 1736, the timber bridge was reconstructed into a single-arch stone bridge, which resembled a rainbow touching the water from afar, hence the name "the Rainbow Bridge". (The Chinese character for "red" and "rainbow" have the same pronunciation) In 1751, a square pavilion was built on top of the bridge, which has long been destroyed by wind and rain erosion.

第一景观。清代很多文人名士都曾来此赏景游玩，并留下了吟咏的诗作。其中一首诗中写道："扬州好，第一是虹桥。杨柳绿齐三尺雨，樱桃红破一声箫，处处驻兰桡。"词中写出了大虹桥初春时节的美景。由于文人们的吟咏，扬州大虹桥声名远播。

- 瘦西湖上的大虹桥
  Big Rainbow Bridge on the Slender West Lake

The Big Rainbow Bridge faces the wide area of the Slender West Lake merging with the beautiful scenery of waves in the water and clouds in the sky. The Willow Causeway (*Liu Di*) to the west of the bridge was constructed in the Sui Dynasty (581-618). During the Qing Dynasty willows and flowers were planted on the Willow Causeway. In the spring, colorful flowers blossom in the midst of willow trees. This scenic beauty is considered the "No. 1 sight in Yangzhou". Many notable scholars who had visited here left memorable poems and writings. One of the poems says that the best of Yangzhou is the Rainbow Bridge where one can see green willows, red cherries and small boats floating on the lake.

> 五亭桥

　　五亭桥又名"莲花桥"，位于江苏扬州莲性寺的莲花堤上，横跨瘦西湖。

　　据记载，五亭桥初建于清乾隆二十二年（1757年）。这一年，乾隆皇帝第二次巡视江南，当地官员

• 初春时节的瘦西湖
Slender West Lake in the Early Spring

> Five Pavilions Bridge (Wuting Qiao)

The Five Pavilions Bridge, also known as "the Lotus Bridge", is situated on the Lotus Causeway of the Lianxing Temple, Yangzhou City, Jiangsu Province across the Slender West Lake. It was originally constructed in 1757. When Emperor

- 瘦西湖上的五亭桥

据说每到月圆之夜，五亭桥下15个桥洞各衔一月，金波荡漾，意境绝佳。

Five Pavilions Bridge on the Slender West Lake

It is said the on a full-moon night, the best night scenery in the Five Pavilions Bridge is the moon reflection under each of the 15 arches.

为讨好皇帝，不惜人力物力，抓紧时间兴修了这座石桥。太平天国时期，桥上的五亭和走廊被火烧毁，光绪年间重修，1933年再次重修。

五亭桥全桥长55.3米，高约8米，平面为"工"字形，两端修有石阶。桥基由12块大青石砌成大小不同的桥墩，桥身为拱券形，由三种不同的券洞联合，共有15个桥孔，中心的券洞跨度最大，四边券洞较小，桥两端的石阶下又各有一个半拱，在厚重的桥基上安排空灵

Qianlong was on his second inspection tour of the south of the Yangtze River, the local officials ordered to build this stone bridge in a short time at the cost of human and material resources in order to win favor from the emperor. Between 1851 and 1864, the five pavilions and the corridor on the bridge were all burned down. The bridge was rebuilt between 1875 and 1908, and reconstructed again in 1933.

The Five Pavilions Bridge is 55.3m long and 8m high with a bridge deck in the shape of the Chinese character "工" with stone stairways on each side. The bridge piles support 12 big and small bluestone piers. The bridge has 15 arches in three different types of spans. The arch in the center of the bridge has the biggest span surrounded by relatively smaller arches on four side sections of the bridge. A semicircular arch sits under the stone stairways. This structure places a flexible arch on the heavy bridge foundation by inserting an arched opening into a straight-line corner.

的拱券，在直线的拼缝转角中安置了曲线的桥洞。居中有一座大亭子，四翼各有一座小亭，五亭均有红色的柱子支撑，设有坐凳栏杆，亭与亭之间有廊相连。亭顶覆有黄色琉璃瓦，亭角飞翘，亭内有彩绘藻井，显得富丽堂皇。

五亭桥的桥基、桥身、桥亭比例恰当，桥基的稳重雄伟与桥亭的玲珑秀丽相结合，风格上既有北方之雄又有南方之秀。

A big pavilion stands in the center of the bridge deck surrounded by four smaller pavilions in the side sections. The five pavilions, connected by corridors, all have supporting red painted pillars and railing seats. The yellow glazed roof tiles, upturned double eaves and color-painted engraved ceilings give them a magnificent and luxurious appearance.

The Five Pavilions Bridge has a proportional layout of the foundations, body and pavilions. The integration between the solid and heavy bridge foundations and delicately designed pavilions demonstrates a combined style of magnificence from the north and elegance from the south.

苏堤与苏堤六桥

苏堤，原名"苏公堤"，是横卧在杭州西湖上的一道堤坝，南起南屏路，北至岳王庙东的曲院风荷，全长2794米，堤面的最宽处为55米，最窄处为18米。苏堤初建于宋元祐四年（1089），著名文学家苏轼当时任杭州知州，他见西湖大半已被泥沙淤塞，残柳稀疏，不堪入目，于是便向朝廷写了奏折，请求疏浚西湖。奏请得到批准后，他便动员了二十多万民工，对西湖大加整治，并用从湖中挖出的淤泥筑成了一道堤坝，使西湖的南岸和北岸可以直接相通。这道堤便被称为"苏公堤"，简称"苏堤"。

堤上的六座桥梁，也始建于宋代，被称为"苏堤六桥"，即映波桥、锁澜桥、望山桥、压堤桥、东浦桥和跨虹桥。北京颐和园中的西堤六桥就是仿照它们的模式修建的。元、明、清时期，苏堤和苏堤六桥又经过多次修整。现在，苏堤六桥依然轻灵优美。

Su Causeway and Its Six Bridges

Su Causeway (*Su Di*), originally Sir Su Causeway, lies across the West Lake in Hangzhou starting from Nanping Street in the south and ending at the Lotus Brewery (*Quyuan Fenghe*) east of the Yuewang Temple in the north. It has a total length of 2,794m with the widest section at 55m and the narrowest at 18m. The causeway was constructed in 1089 during the Song Dynasty when the renowned litterateur Su Shi was a Hangzhou magistrate. When he witnessed the unsightly scene of the mostly silted West Lake and dying willow trees, Su Shi submitted a proposal to the imperial court requesting to dredge up the silt from the West Lake. When his proposal was approved, he mobilized over 200,000 workers to clean up the West Lake. The silt from the West Lake was used to build the causeway connecting the south riverbanks to the north riverbanks of the West Lake. The causeway was then named "Sir Su Causeway" or simply "Su Causeway".

Six bridges were built on the Su Causeway in the Song Dynasty: Ripple Reflection Bridge (*Yingbo Qiao*), Locking Waves Bridge (*Suolan Qiao*), Lookout Mountain Bridge (*Wangshan Qiao*), Over Causeway Bridge (*Yadi Qiao*), East Bay Bridge (*Dongpu Qiao*) and Crossing Rainbow Bridge

- 苏堤映波桥
Ripple Reflection Bridge (*Yingbo Qiao*)

(*Kuahong Qiao*). The six bridges on the West Causeway in the Summer Palace in Beijing are imitations of these six bridges on the Su Causeway. Both Su Causeway and the six bridges went through many repairs in the Yuan, Ming and Qing dynasties. Today, they still look delicate and elegant.

● 苏堤风光
The Scenery of Su Causeway

> 断桥

　　断桥位于浙江杭州西湖环湖北路和白堤之间，横跨在内西湖和外西湖的分水线上。西湖著名的"断桥残雪"的景色指的就是这里。

　　断桥初建的确切年代已不可考，不过唐代诗人张祜的《题杭州孤山寺》一诗中就有"断桥"一词，说明最晚在唐代断桥就已

> Broken Bridge *(Duan Qiao)*

The Broken Bridge is situated on the dividing line across the inner and outer West Lake between the Bai Causeway and the North West Lake Ring Road in Hangzhou, Zhejiang Province, best known as the "Lingering Snow on Broken Bridge" sight on the West Lake.

　　The year of the bridge's original construction is unknown. But a poem titled *On Hangzhou's Solitary Hill (Gushan) Temple* by Tang-dynasty poet

- **西湖断桥**

  西湖三面环山，一面临市，是一座椭圆形的大湖。苏堤和白堤把它分为内湖、外湖、岳湖、西里湖和小南湖五个部分。断桥所处的位置恰好在西湖风景线上。游人走在桥上，青山绿水和湖中诸岛的景观尽收眼底。

  Broken Bridge on the West Lake

  The West Lake is a huge oval-shaped lake surrounded by mountains on three sides and Hangzhou City on one side. The Su and Bai Causeways divide the lake into five areas: the inner West Lake, the outer West Lake, Yue Lake, West Inner (*Xili*) Lake and Little South (*Xiaonan*) Lake. The Broken Bridge is located right on the West Lake scenic route. Standing on the bridge, visitors can enjoy a panoramic view of the surrounding mountains, the water and all the islands on the lake.

建成。到了元代，桥名为"段家桥""短桥"。由于从孤山来的白堤到此中断，又因为"段""断"谐音，所以又作"断桥"。现在的断桥是一座堤障式单孔石拱桥，桥面两侧设有青石栏杆，风貌古朴淡雅。桥东堍有清代康熙帝御题的"断桥残雪"碑亭，亭侧建有水

Zhang Hu mentions the Broken Bridge, which proves that the bridge had already been built in the Tang Dynasty. In the Yuan Dynasty, the bridge was called "Duan Family Bridge" (*Duanjia Qiao*) or "Short Bridge" (*Duan Qiao*). The name "Broken Bridge" (*Duan Qiao*) derives from the fact that the route from the Solitary Hill (*Gu Shan*) to Bai Causeway ended here and also from the same pronunciation of the character *Duan* ("段") referring to a family name and the character *Duan* ("断") meaning broken. The current bridge is a single-arch stone bridge in a causeway style, bluestone railings on each side of the bridge. The bridge has a classic simple structure. At the east end of the bridge stands a stele in a pavilion with the inscriptions "Lingering Snow on the Broken Bridge" by Emperor Kangxi of

- **"断桥残雪"碑亭**

冬季大雪初霁之时，白堤和岸边银装素裹，唯断桥桥顶积雪早融，灰色桥面与湖水色调一致，似乎白堤至此已断，景观独特。"断桥残雪"说的就是这种景观。

"Lingering Snow on the Broken Bridge" Stele Pavilion

The phrase "Lingering Snow on the Broken Bridge" describes a unique sight in the winter when the Bai Causeway and the riverbanks are all covered with white snow, except for the deck of the Broken Bridge on which the snow has already started to melt. The gray color of the bridge deck seems to match the cold water in the lake as if the Bai Causeway was broken up at this location.

榭，题额"云水光中"，青瓦朱栏，飞檐翘角，与桥、亭构成了一幅古意盎然的风景画。

the Qing Dynasty. A horizontal tablet hung on the top of the waterside pavilion says "In the Light of Water and Clouds", which implies that this beautiful pavilion looks like an ancient landscape painting with a bluestone roof, red painted railings, upturned eaves and raised corners.

白堤

白堤原名"白沙堤"，是唐朝时为了贮蓄湖水灌溉农田而兴建，横亘在西湖东西向的湖面上，从断桥起，过锦带桥，止于平湖秋月，长1公里。唐代诗人白居易任杭州刺史时有诗云："最爱湖东行不足，绿杨荫里白沙堤。"说的就是此堤。宋代时，因为这条长堤是通往孤山的唯一道路，故称"孤山路"。明代，堤上广植碧桃和垂柳，又称"十锦塘"。现在的白堤上桃柳成行，芳草如茵，远近青山绿水，行人如在画中游。

Bai Causeway

The White Causeway was originally called the "White Sand Causeway" built in the Tang Dynasty to store and control water for farmland irrigation. It lies across the West Lake from east to west starting at the Broken Bridge, through the Brocade Belt Bridge and ending at the "Moon over the Peaceful Lake in Autumn" sight reaching a total length of one kilometer. The famous Tang-dynasty poet Bai Juyi, who was once a Hangzhou magistrate, mentioned this causeway in his poem that he never felt enough walking in the east side of West Lake on the White Sand Causeway amidst lush greens. In the Song Dynasty, the causeway became the only road to the Solitary Hills, hence the name "Solitary Hill Road" at the time. In the Ming Dynasty, many willows and peach trees were planted on the causeway, which was called the "Variety Lakeside". Today on the Bai Causeway, visitors enjoy a view of lines of willow and peach trees against distant mountains and gorgeous water as if one was walking in a beautiful painting.

• 白居易像
Portrait of Poet Bai Juyi

> 拱宸桥

拱宸桥位于浙江杭州市内的大关桥之北，东西横跨大运河，是京杭大运河到杭州的终点标志，也是杭州古桥中最高最长的石拱桥。拱宸桥始建于明崇祯四年（1631年），由当时一个名叫祝华封的举人募集资金建造。清顺治八年（1651年），桥因故坍塌，康熙五十三年（1714年）得以重修。在古代，"宸"是指帝王居住之所，"拱"即两手相合表示敬意。"拱宸桥"的桥名代表了皇帝南巡时对皇帝的相迎和尊崇之意。

桥长98米，高16米，桥面中段略窄，而两端桥堍处有12.2米宽。桥身用条石砌筑，桥面呈柔和的弧线形，桥下为三孔薄墩，桥形巍峨高大，气魄雄伟。

> Gongchen Bridge

The Gongchen Bridge is situated in the Hangzhou city, Zhejiang Province north of the Daguan Bridge across the Grand Canal from east to west. It marks the final destination of the Beijing-Hangzhou Grand Canal. It is also the tallest and the longest stone arch bridge among the ancient bridges in Hangzhou. The original construction started in 1631 financed by a scholar named Zhu Huafeng. The bridge collapsed in 1651 and was rebuilt in 1714. In ancient Chinese, *Chen* refers to the residence of emperors or kings and *Gong* means putting the palms of two hands together to show respect. The name "Gongchen Bridge" represented greetings and respect for the emperor during his inspection visits to the south of the Yangtze River.

The Bridge is 98m long and 16m tall. The deck is a little narrower in the middle and 12.2m wide at each end of the bridge. The bridge deck is paved with stone blocks forming a gentle slope. There are three arches on thin-wall piers. The bridge has a majestic towering profile.

• 拱宸桥（图片提供：FOTOE）
Gongchen Bridge

> 八字桥

八字桥位于浙江绍兴城区八字桥直街的东端。据史书记载，此桥始建于南宋嘉泰年间，南宋宝祐四年（1256年）重建。八字桥为梁式石桥，东西走向，桥洞宽4.5米，桥长约4.8米。这座桥坐落在三街三河的交叉处，行人上下桥所走的踏跺分三面四道，与三条道路相贯通。桥东为南、北落坡，成八字形，桥西为西、南落坡，成"八"字形；桥两端的南向两个落坡也成"八"字形，且坡下各有一个桥洞，由此又形成了两座小桥。这种桥坡结构在中国古桥中十分少见，被专家称为"古代的立交桥"。

> Bazi Bridge

The Bazi Bridge (*Bazi* means character eight "八") is situated at the east end of the Bazi Bridge Street in Shaoxing, Zhejiang Province. According to historical records, it was built between 1201 and 1204, and rebuilt in 1256 during the Southern Song Dynasty. It is a stone beam bridge from east to west, 4.5m wide and around 4.8m long. Located at an intersection of three rivers and three streets, the bridge deck has four stairways facing three directions connecting to three roads. The east section of the bridge deck has two slopes, one to the south and the other to the north forming a shape of the character "八"; the west section has two slopes, one to the west and one to the south forming another "八"; and the two ends of the bridge has two slopes to the south forming yet another "八". Under each slope of the bridge end there is an arch, which looks like a smaller bridge of its own. This kind of structural design for the bridge deck is rarely seen in Chinese ancient bridges. Therefore this bridge is called by bridge experts as an "ancient overpass".

- 浙江绍兴八字桥

  桥下石壁转角处犹有被船只纤绳磨出的痕迹，可见当年桥下舟楫之盛。

  Bazi Bridge in Shaoxing City, Zhejiang Province

  In the corner of the stone wall under the bridge, the tow-rope grind marks can still be seen, which shows the busy boat traffic in the past.

> 熟溪桥

熟溪桥位于浙江武义县城南，南北向横跨熟溪。此桥始建于南宋开禧三年（1207），历史上曾多次毁于洪水和大火，又屡修屡建。现桥为木石结构的伸臂式梁桥，桥上有桥屋，成为最早的风雨廊桥之一。熟溪桥全长140米，桥面宽4.80米，通高13.40米，九孔十墩，迎水面砌有分水尖，墩高4.40米。桥屋共有49间，中设重檐歇山顶的亭阁三间。桥面两侧间隔设有条凳，供游人休息。条凳将廊桥分成三道，古时两旁走行人，中间通车马。桥身两旁设有独具江南特色的木栏杆，倚栏远眺，可尽览小城的美景。

> Shuxi Bridge

The Shuxi Bridge is situated in the south of Wuyi County, Zhejiang Province across the Shuxi River from south to north. Originally constructed in 1207 in the Song Dynasty, it went through destructions by flood and fire and many rebuilding. The current bridge is a covered cantilever beam bridge of stone and timber. It is one of the oldest so-called "corridor" bridges to protect pedestrians from wind and rain. It has a total length of 140m, a deck width of 4.80m and a general height of 13.40m. There are nine arches and ten 4.40m high piers with a watershed on the side facing the water flow. The bridge deck has a total of 49 covered sections including three pavilions with double-eave roofs of classical Chinese architectural style. The benches on the bridge divide the deck into three ways, the middle one for

- 武义熟溪桥

   熟溪桥中间的二层八角楼阁名为"法角亭"，亭柱上有浮雕的鸟兽人物，栩栩如生。

   Shuxi Bridge in Wuyi County

   The two-story octagonal building in the center of the Shuxi Bridge is called Fajiao Pavilion, which has vivid images of animals and human figures embossed on the pavilion pillars.

carriages and the two on each side for pedestrians in ancient times. The railings are wood rails in the style typical of the regions south of the Yangtze River. Visitors can enjoy a beautiful view of the small town from the bridge.

伸臂式梁桥

　　中国南方比较常见的木梁桥，往往都属于伸臂式梁桥。也就是在修建桥梁时从两岸同时开工，以长且大的木头层层相压，每一层都比下面一层伸出一些，到河中心两头相接，远看像两条伸出的手臂相握。由于木质桥梁在风雨侵蚀下易于腐朽，人们往往又在桥上建屋作亭，称"风雨桥"或"廊桥"。

Cantilever Beam Bridge

Most of the beam bridges in South China are cantilever beam bridges. Basically the construction begins simultaneously from both ends of the bridge by laying beams one level at a time with the longer beam always above the shorter one and eventually connecting the beams at the top level in the center. From afar this structure looks like two arms reaching out to each other. Since rain erosion happens easily on timber beam bridges, the bridge decks are often covered or built with pavilions on top. These covered bridges are called "Wind and Rain Bridges" or "Corridor Bridges".

- 西藏地区的藏式伸臂桥
  A Zang-style Cantilever Bridge in Xizang

> 彩虹桥

彩虹桥位于江西婺源清华镇，横跨在清华河上。此桥始建于宋代，桥名取自唐代大诗人李白（701—762）诗作《秋登宣城谢朓北楼》中的名句"两水夹明镜，双桥落彩虹"。桥长140米，桥面宽3米多，桥下有4墩5孔，每墩上建有一个桥亭，西亭之间为桥廊，廊亭中有石桌石凳。

桥墩像半个船形，前面锋锐，

> Rainbow Bridge (Caihong Qiao)

The Rainbow Bridge crosses the Qinghua River in Qinghua Town, Wuyuan County, Jiangxi Province. Originally constructed in the Song Dynasty, the bridge was named after a well-known verse by Tang-dynasty poet Li Bai (701-762) that says, "A bright mirror between two waters, a rainbow falling over two bridges." It is 140m long with a deck width of over 3 meters. There are 5 openings and 4 piers with a pavilion standing on each of the piers. Between

- 彩虹桥上的"长虹卧波"横匾
  The Horizontal Tablet "Rainbow over Ripples" on the Rainbow Bridge

后面平整，可以分解洪水对桥墩的冲击力。一般来说，各桥墩之间距离相等比较美观，但彩虹桥墩距的最大跨度为12.8米，最小的为9.8米，相差近6米。这种设定是根据汛期河面洪水的流速变化确定的。河面流速最快的地方墩距较大，有利于行洪；而流速缓的地方则墩距较小。

- **婺源彩虹桥**

彩虹桥周围景色优美，青山如黛，碧水澄清，坐在这里稍作休憩，浏览四周风光，会让人深深体验到婺源之美。

Rainbow Bridge in Wuyuan County

The enchanting scenery of green mountains and clear water around the Rainbow Bridge leaves visitors a deep impression of Wuyuan's beauty.

every two pavilions there is a corridor with stone tables and chairs inside.

The boat-shaped bridge piers with a pointed front and a flat back can relieve the pressure from the floodwater. Usually it looks better if the piers have the same distance between each other. But the Rainbow Bridge has a largest span of 12.8m and a smallest span of 9.8m having a 6m difference. This is decided by the water flow velocity during the flood season, a longer distance for more rapid water flow and a shorter distance for lower velocity.

> 万年桥

万年桥在江西南城县东北的歇洋渡，横跨于抚河之上。这座桥是江西省境内最长的一座古代联拱石桥。万年桥初建于南宋咸淳七年（1271年），当时是一座浮桥。明崇祯十年（1637年）重建为石桥，到清顺治四年（1647年）方才完工，工期横跨明、清两代，长达12年，其中大半时间花在第18墩上。因为这里有一深潭，潭深流急，漩涡重重。桥墩在建造时采用了排水施工的干修法，曾聚集民工数万，修建围堰，挡洪引水，填石为基，并在石缝之间填以卵石、沙土和石灰，然后再在桥基上修拱券、铺面石。这种方法在古代桥梁的修建中尚不多见。

万年桥全长411米，桥面宽5.8

> Thousand-Year Bridge (Wannian Qiao)

The Thousand-Year Bridge is situated at Xieyang Crossing northeast of Nancheng County, Jiangxi Province across the Fu River. It is the longest stone bridge of continuous spans in Jiangxi Province. First constructed as a floating bridge in 1271, it was rebuilt into a stone bridge in 1637 and completed in 1647 taking a total of 12 years in two dynasties. Most of the time was spent on the 18th bridge pier at a location with a deep whirlpool under the water. Tens of thousands of migrant workers were mobilized to build a cofferdam to block the flood, pump the water out and fill up with rocks for the bridge foundation. Rock crevices were filled with small pebbles, sand and lime. The arches and the bridge deck were built on top of the man-made bridge foundation. This construction method

米，桥高20米。全桥共有桥洞23个，其跨度为14米。此桥桥基坚实，桥身轻巧，桥墩的前墩尖而高昂，后墩方而低矮，有昂首挺胸迎水之势。

was rarely seen in bridge building in ancient times.

The Thousand-Year Bridge is 411m long, 5.8m wide and 20m tall with 23 arches, each arch spanning 14 meters. The bridge foundation is strong and solid supporting a relatively light body. The bridge pier has a high pointed front and low flat back as if it raises its head high to welcome the water.

• 南城歇洋渡上的万年桥（图片提供：FOTOE）
Thousand-Year Bridge in Xieyang Crossing of Nancheng County

> 三峡桥

三峡桥位于江西省庐山南麓的石人峰下，南北横跨于三峡涧上。这条山涧怪石嶙峋，山崖陡峭，涧水奔腾，酷如长江三峡，北宋文学家苏轼（1037—1101）将其称为"三峡涧"，而桥也因此而得名"三峡桥"。又因涧西有栖贤寺，三峡桥又名"栖贤桥"。

从桥下的券石上刻着的文字可知，三峡桥始建于宋大中祥符七年（1014年），是由江西的僧人文秀和福建的僧人德朗主持修建的，而石桥的建造者是陈智福等工匠。清道光年间，桥头处建了一座观音阁，三峡桥被称为"观音桥"。桥下的石栏杆就是观音阁的僧人募化修建的。

三峡桥是一座单孔石拱桥，

> Three Gorges Bridge

The Three Gorges Bridge is under the Stone Man Peak (*Shiren Feng*) at the southern foot of Lushan Mountain, Jiangxi Province. It crosses from south to north the Three Gorges Gully with grotesque rock, steep cliffs and raging water flow, a place that very much resembles the Three Gorges in the Yangtze River. The famous writer Su Shi (1037-1101) of the Northern Song Dynasty called it "Three Gorges Gully", hence the name "Three Gorges Bridge". It was also known as "Qixian Bridge" named after the Qixian Temple to the west of the gully.

According to the inscriptions on a stone arch, the bridge was originally constructed in 1014 during the Song Dynasty under the supervision of Monk Wenxiu from Jiangxi Province and Monk Delang from Fujian Province. The bridge

● 庐山三峡桥（图片提供：全景正片）
Three Gorges Bridge in Lushan Mountain

全桥用107块石料砌筑而成，全长20.4米，桥面宽4.94米，桥洞跨径为10.33米。桥的两端以山石为基，因受地形影响，南高北低。此桥建成后，千年以来，任凭桥下的三峡涧水狂奔撞击，桥身今天仍安然无恙，可见桥梁建造技术之高超。

builders were a group of stonemasons headed by Chen Zhifu. Between 1821 and 1850, the Bodhisattva Guanyin Pavilion was built at the bridgehead. Therefore the bridge was also known as the Bodhisattva Guanyin Bridge. The bridge railings were financed by alms collected by monks in the Bodhisattva Guanyin Pavilion.

The Three-Gorges Bridge is a single-arch stone bridge made of 107 stone slabs at 20.4m long and 4.94m wide with a 10.33m span. The bridge used the mountain rocks as its abutments. The topography causes the north bridge end higher than the south bridge end. Over a thousand years after it was built, the bridge still stands firm no matter how big the impact the raging water flow in the gully has bronght, thanks to the superb bridge building techniques.

- 清奇秀丽的庐山风光
  Gorgeous Scenery of Lushan Mountain

> 渌水桥

渌水桥位于湖南醴陵城南，横跨在渌水河上。据史料记载，渌水桥初建于南宋宝祐年间。当时的渌水桥为一座伸臂木梁桥，有7个石桥墩。其后的元、明、清历代又经过数次重修。其中明代成化九年（1473年）重修时，人们在桥上修建了桥屋；万历三十四年（1606年），桥上建屋百间，桥中间更是建起一座楼，楼内供奉真武大帝的神像。到了清代，人们在桥上修建板亭数十间，渌水桥便成了当时的一个贸易中心，桥上店铺连绵，人声鼎沸。不过现在桥面上的这些贸易建筑均已不存，仅供人们通行。

现在的渌水桥是1928年重修时的遗物，是一座拥有十扎桥洞的联拱石桥，长203米，宽5.3米。南北两

> Lushui Bridge

The Lushui Bridge crosses the Lushui River to the south of Liling, Hunan Province. According to historical records, it was initially constructed between 1253 and 1258 in the Southern Song Dynasty. Originally it was a cantilever bridge made of timber beam with 7 stone piers. After many times of rebuilding during the Yuan, Ming and Qing dynasties, a few covered sections were added on the bridge in the 1473 during the Ming Dynasty. By 1606 over a hundred covered sections were finished including a multi-story building in the middle of the bridge. A statue of Emperor Zhenwu is enshrined inside the building. By the Qing Dynasty dozens of wooden booths were set up on the bridge deck making the Lushui Bridge a bustling trade center crowded with many shops and people. The shops no longer existed and the

端设引桥，桥面、桥栏杆全部用麻石砌成。桥侧有清末维新派领袖康有为题写的"渌江桥"三字，与醴陵文人傅熊湘撰写的《渌江桥记》碑文。

- 湖南醴陵渌水桥
  Lushui Bridge of Liling City, Hunan Province

bridge only serves as a walkway for pedestrians.

The current bridge is the relic of the one reconstruction in 1928. It is a 203m long and 5.3m wide stone bridge with ten arches of continuous spans and an approach on each end of the bridge. The bridge deck and railings are all made of granite. The side of the bridge has the bridge's name inscribed by Kang Youwei, the leading reformer in the late Qing Dynasty and a stele inscribed by Fu Xiongxiang, a scholar from Liling documenting the history of the bridge.

> 龙脑桥

龙脑桥位于四川泸县的九曲河上，始建于明洪武年间，为石墩石梁式平桥，全长55米，高约2米，宽1.9米，共有桥墩14座，由四层灰沙岩石条垒砌而成。此桥既未用榫卯衔接，也未用粘接物填缝，全靠各构件本身相互垒砌承托，在建筑技术上达到了很高的水平。

龙脑桥的石雕工艺精湛娴熟，夸张与写实相结合，风格浑厚刚毅，造型生动，为中国古桥中的罕见之作。桥下中间四个桥墩上各雕一条巨龙，龙头上的眼、耳、口、鼻、眉、髯、角，龙身上的鳞甲、双翅和流云都雕刻得线条明快，清晰流畅。龙口内有一颗用整石镂雕而成的石球，重达30多千克，可滚动自如，但又不能取出。巨龙左右

> Loong Head Bridge *(Longnao Qiao)*

The Loong Head Bridge crosses the Jiuqu River in Luxian County, Sichuan Province. Constructed between 1368 and 1398 during the Ming Dynasty, this bridge of stone beams and piers is 55m long, 2m high and 1.9m wide with 14 stone piers made of four layers of gray sand stone bricks. No mortise and tenon or bonding materials were used. All the bridge components were assembled and locked together showing a very high level of craftsmanship.

The exquisite stone carvings on the Loong Head Bridge are a masterpiece of perfect integration of artistic realism and exaggerations in a vivid and masculine style rarely seen among Chinese ancient bridges. On each of the four piers stands a huge stone loong with skillfully carved eyes, ears, mouth, nose, eyebrows and

两边的桥墩上，又依次雕有雄狮、大象、麒麟，均雄姿勃勃，气势昂然。龙、狮、象、麒麟的形体在桥面上露头，桥面下现尾，如果遇到河水上涨淹没桥板时，这些神兽水中只露出头和尾，就像在河中遨游一样，可谓奇观。

horns as well as scales, wings and lines on the loong body. A 30-kilogram ball carved from a complete stone block rolls freely inside the mouth of the loong, but it is impossible to take it out. On each side of the loong pier there are stone sculptures of vigorous images of lions, elephants and kylins. With their heads above the deck and tails below the deck, these mythical beasts look like they were swimming in the river when the deck is submerged by rising water.

• 龙脑桥上的石雕（图片提供：FOTOE）
Stone Carvings on the Loong Head Bridge

> 安澜桥

安澜桥也称"珠浦桥",位于四川都江堰。此桥通过分水鱼嘴横跨在岷江的内外江上,原为一座竹索桥,现已改建成钢索桥。

安澜桥的初建年代史书上没有记载,但可以肯定在宋代以前就有了,初时名为"珠浦桥"。当时的桥共有5个桥墩,并且是用木桩和石头筑成的。明朝末年,当地官府为阻止张献忠领导的农民起义军,拆掉了索桥,从此人们过河只能坐船。由于这里是成都平原通往川西北的必经之路,来往行人众多,仅靠渡船难以满足需求,而且江宽水急,沉船惨剧时有发生,过渡者苦不堪言。清嘉庆八年(1803年),私塾先生何先德夫妇因目睹惨烈的渡船倾覆事故,决心为民造福,重

> Anlan Bridge

The Anlan Bridge, also known as the Zhupu Bridge, is situated at Dujiangyan City, Sichuan Province across the Fish Mouth Levee of the Minjiang River. It was originally a bamboo cable suspension bridge and later changed to a steel cable suspension bridge.

Although no historical records documented the year of its original construction, the bridge seems to have existed before the Song Dynasty with the name "Zhupu Bridge". The bridge then had five piers built in both timber and stone. By the end of the Ming Dynasty, the bridge was dismantled by the local government to stop the peasant uprising army led by Zhang Xianzhong. After that people could only cross the river by boat. Since this was the only route from the Chengdu Plain to northwest of Sichuan, ferryboats could hardly meet the needs of many travelers.

修索桥。他们拿出多年积蓄，并四处募集，筹足了资金；又参照古人对索桥的记载，设计了建桥方案，制作了新桥模型，招工备料，动工建桥。桥尚未完工时，有两个樵夫不顾劝阻，顶风过桥，落水丧生。渡口的恶霸买通官府，诬告何先德以草菅人命之罪，将其害死。何妻强压悲愤，继承大志，最终完成了

- **都江堰安澜索桥**（图片提供：FOTOE）
安澜桥远看如飞虹挂空，十分别致。漫步桥上，西望岷江穿山咆哮而来，东望灌渠纵横，整个都江堰的概貌尽收眼底。

Anlan Bridge in Dujiangyan
From afar, the Anlan Bridge looks like a rainbow in the sky. When walking on the bridge, one can enjoy a panoramic view of Dujiangyan with the raging water of the Minjiang River coming towards the bridge from the west and the entire irrigation system in the east.

In addition, due to rapid water flow in the river, tragedies of boats sunken were not uncommon. In 1803 during the Qing Dynasty, a school teacher named Kong Xiande and his wife having witnessed the tragic event of an overturned ferryboat, determined to rebuild the suspension bridge for the local people. They not only donated their money savings of many years, but also went out to raise enough funds for the bridge construction. They designed a plan and made a new bridge model based on the historical documentations about building suspension bridges. With the building materials prepared and workers hired, the bridge construction started. But before the bridge was completed, two woodcutters tried to cross the bridge against the big wind, but fell into the river drowned. Some ferryboat bullies bribed the local officials to kill He Xiande on the false accusation that he neglected human life when building the bridge. Luckily, his wife overcame her sadness and fulfilled her husband's will by completing the construction of the suspension bridge with plank paved bridge deck and bamboo railings. The bridge was named Anlan Bridge

● 都江堰渠首俯瞰（图片提供：FOTOE）
Overlooking the Irrigation System of Dujiangyan

索桥的修建。桥上横铺木板，以竹缆为栏，取名"安栏桥"，后改"安澜桥"，取不畏波澜之意。人们感激何先德夫妻的功德，又称此桥为"夫妻桥"。

安澜桥共有八孔九墩，其中最中间的桥墩为石墩，其余八墩为木桩石固墩。全桥共有粗长竹索24根，其中10根为底索，上铺木板，构成桥面，木板上有两根竹索用来压住木板；另外12根为扶栏索，分列于桥的两旁。桥两头各有一间石

meaning not to be afraid of raging water. To express their gratefulness to He Xiande and his wife, local people also called it "the Husband and Wife Bridge".

The Anlan Bridge has eight openings and nine piers, among which the one in the middle is a stone pier and the rest wooden piers reinforced by stone. There used to be 24 long and thick bamboo cables including ten cables used as the base for the bridge roadway with planks laid on top. Two additional bamboo cables were added to press down the planks. Another twelve cables were used as rails on each side of the

室，里面的木笼中安装着绞索设备，可以绞紧桥的底索和扶栏索。由于竹索太长，从两头绞紧非常困难，所以桥梁中间的石墩上增设了一套绞索设备，也置于石室木笼中，木笼上面建有桥亭。

1975年，在兴修分水鱼嘴外江闸的时候，安澜桥被下移了一百米，竹索同时被换成了钢绳，木架石固桥墩被换成了钢筋混凝土墩，桥栏也被换成了钢筋混凝土构件。全桥长3401米，宽1.4米，高14米。

bridge. At each end of the bridge a stone room was built to anchor the suspender placed inside a wooden cage to tighten both the suspension and the railing cables. Because of the very long length of the bamboo cables, an additional suspender was anchored in the middle pier. The suspender is also placed in a wooden cage inside of a stone room, but with a pavilion built on top.

In 1975 while building the Fish Mouth Levee, the bridge was moved 100 meters downwards. The bamboo cables were changed to steel cables, and the stone-reinforced wooden piers were changed to reinforced concrete piers. The bamboo rails were also replaced with steel bars. This suspension bridge is now 3,401m long, 1.4m wide and 14m high.

古老的水利工程——都江堰

都江堰位于今四川省都江堰市，岷江中游。工程始建于公元前250年，渠首在灌县境内，包括"鱼嘴""金刚堤""飞沙堰"和"宝瓶口"四个主要工程和数以千计的渠道与分堰。鱼嘴是修建在江心的分水堤坝，把汹涌的岷江分隔成外江和内江，外江用于排洪，内江用于引水灌溉。飞沙堰起泄洪、排沙和调节水量的作用。宝瓶口因形状犹如瓶颈而得名，作用是控制内江的进水流量。内江的水经过宝瓶口流入川西平原灌溉农田。整个工程将岷江水一分为二，既解除了岷江水患，又使成都平原获得灌溉与运输之利，成都平原自此成为真正的"天府之国"。作为世界上年代最久并使用至今的大型水利工程，都江堰被誉为"世界水利文化的鼻祖"。

Ancient Irrigation System—Dujiangyan

Dujiangyan is situated in Dujiangyan City, Sichuan Province in the Minjiang River midstream. The construction started in 250 B.C. to build the head works in the Guanxian County including the four major projects of the Fish Mouth Levee (*Yuzui*), Jingang Causeway, Flying Sand Dam (*Feishayan*) and Bottleneck Channel (*Baopingkou*) and thousands of other channels and smaller dams. Built in the middle of the Minjiang River, the Fish Mouth is a levee that divides the water into inner stream for farmland irrigation and outer stream to release floods. The Flying Sand Dam is built to release overflow of floodwaters, discharge sediment and regulate the water volume. The Bottleneck Channel derives its name from its narrow shape like a bottleneck and is responsible for controlling the influent flow of the inner stream for farmland irrigation west of Sichuan. The Minjiang River is divided into two by the whole Dujiangyan construction, which not only resolved the flooding problems, but also facilitated irrigation and transportation for the Chengdu Plain, which became a real "land of abundance" in Sichuan after Dujiangyan project was completed. As a large irrigation system used in the longest time in the world, Dujiangyan is acclaimed the "originator of the world's water conservation culture".

都江堰宝瓶口（图片提供：FOTOE）
Bottleneck Channel of Dujiangyan

> 泸定桥

泸定桥又名"大渡河铁索桥",位于四川省泸定县城西,横跨于波涛汹涌的大渡河上。

泸定桥所在的地区,是通往康定等藏族、彝族聚居区的重要通道。这里东有二郎山,西有大雪山,两山夹峙,一水中流,交通十分不便。过去人们只能靠牛皮筏渡河,或通过竹索、藤索溜渡。清康熙年间,清兵平定了当地土司的叛乱,为满足经济发展的需要,在地势稍平、水流稍缓的地方修成了这座铁索桥,工程始自康熙四十四年(1705年),历时两年方才竣工。

泸定桥长104米,桥面宽3米,高14.5米,是用13根铁索组建而成的。其中底索9根,索间距离为33厘米。底索上面铺着横木板,木板上

> Luding Bridge

The Luding Bridge, also known as the "Dadu River Iron Cable Suspension Bridge", is situated west of Luding City, Sichuan Province crossing the raging Dadu River.

The area around the Luding Bridge is a key passageway to Kangding inhabited by Zang and Yi ethnic groups. With only one river flowing through a valley between Erlang Mountain (*Erlang Shan*) and Big Snow Mountain (*Daxue Shan*) it made transportation and traveling very difficult. In the old days people relied on leather rafts or bamboo and rattan rope slides to cross the river. During the reign of Emperor Kangxi of the Qing Dynasty, the Qing-dynasty army put down the rebellion of the local chieftains and built this iron cable suspension bridge in a relatively flatter area with slow water flow to meet the

又铺着八道纵向的走道板,中间四道,两侧各两道,以通行人马。另外的4条铁索分置于桥面两侧,每侧两根,作为扶栏。泸定桥上的铁索每根都有碗口粗,并都是用扁圆形的铁环组成,13根总重21吨,再加上其他的铁木构件,全桥的重量达40吨。在泸定桥的两端各建有一座石砌桥台,高约20米,台内修有落井,井底安有桩锚和地龙桩。泸定桥的13根铁索就分别铆接在这些地龙桩上。两座桥台上还各有桥亭一

needs of local economic development. The construction took two years and the bridge was completed in 1705.

The Luding Bridge is 104m long, 3m wide and 14.5m high. It comprises 13 iron cables, of which 9 cables, 33cm apart from each other, are used for the bridge roadway where planks are placed horizontally on top. Over the horizontal planks additional wood boards are laid out vertically as eight walkways for carriages and pedestrians: four in the middle and two on each side. The other four iron chains are used as railings, two on each side of the bridge. Each cable

• 大渡河上的泸定桥(图片提供:全景正片)
Luding Bridge on Dadu River

座。桥亭既可以保护落井和地龙桩免受雨水侵蚀，同时又是当时的管理者控制通行和征收税款的地方。桥头悬挂着康熙帝题写的"泸定桥"三字的匾，桥东耸立的是康熙帝写的《御制泸定桥碑记》，可见当时朝廷对此桥的重视。

consists of oblate-shape strands as big as a big bowl in diameter. The 13 iron cables have a total weight of 21 tons and the entire bridge weighs 40 tons with additional components. On each side of the bridge there is a 20m high stone tower, which houses a deep well with piles and pile anchors at the bottom of it. The 13 cables are anchored and riveted on these piles. In addition, a pavilion-type of structure sits on top of this tower to protect the equipment from rain erosion. This pavilion was also used by the bridge administration to monitor the traffic and collect taxes in the old days. A horizontal tablet is hung on the bridgehead with the name "Luding Bridge" inscribed by Emperor Kangxi of the Qing Dynasty. In the east of the bridge stands a stele with the inscriptions about the building process of the bridge written by Emperor Kangxi demonstrating the attention given by the imperial court to this bridge.

- 泸定桥桥头大门（图片提供：全景正片）

泸定桥建成后，成为四川内地通往青藏高原的重要通道，而泸定县也很快成为商贸繁荣的市镇。在桥的东岸，曾是边茶交换麝香、皮毛、药材的市场，吸引了许多藏族商贩从康定来到这里交易。

Bridgehead Gateway of Luding Bridge

After its completion the Luding Bridge became the key passageway from the inland of Sichuan to Qinghai-Tibet Plateau. As a result, Luding County grew into a prosperous town of commerce and trade. In the east side of the bridge, the trading market for musk, fur and medicinal herbs attracted many Zang merchants from Kangding to exchange goods here.

> ## 霁虹桥

霁虹桥，又名"澜津桥"，位于云南永平与保山的交界处，是中国乃至世界上现存修建时间最早的一座铁索桥。

在古代，从永平的博南山修建栈道，经澜津渡口，过澜沧江，直到保山，这是内地通往滇西的一条

> ## Rainbow Bridge *(Jihong Qiao)*

The Rainbow Bridge, also known as Lanjin Bridge, is situated at the junction between Yongping County and Baoshan City in Yunnan Province. It is the oldest iron cable suspension bridge existing today in China and in the world.

A plank path in Bonan Mountain

- 云南永平霁虹桥
  Rainbow Bridge in Yongping County, Yunnan Province

交通要道。再从保山西南行，便可到达缅甸、印度，乃至西亚和欧洲。这条古道的开通时间，比河西走廊上的丝绸之路还早。

唐代时，澜津桥为一座竹索桥，元代元贞元年（1295年）改建成木桥，更名为"霁虹桥"。明初桥毁，成化年间，铁索桥得以重修。此后，此桥屡毁屡修，现存的铁索桥为清康熙二十年（1681年）重建，康熙帝曾为此桥亲题"虹飞彼岸"，东岸为此特建有"御书楼"。

霁虹桥高悬于澜沧江上，西岸为陡崖，东岸是险峰，桥下江深水急，一桥飞跨，气势壮观。霁虹桥长113.4米，桥面宽3.7米，全桥由18根铁索组成。承重底链为16根，另有两根为扶手，每边用30根铁条将扶手索和外边底索之间连接起来，形成栏杆状。底部每隔6米左右有一道铁夹板，将16根底索锁住，上铺横板，用铅丝绑扎在铁链上，各板之间再用木条把牢。桥两端筑成半圆形桥台，铁索两头铆死在两岸的桥台上，下面是滔滔江水，十分险要。两边桥头各有一亭，过去在桥的两端还各建有一座关楼，现在西关楼已毁，仅剩东关楼。

of Yongping, through Lanjing crossing and across Lancang River to Baoshan served as a key route of transportation to west Yunnan Province. This ancient road could also lead to Myanmar, India, West Asia and even Europe. It was open earlier than the Silk Road of the Hexi Corridor in Gansu Province.

In the Tang Dynasty, the Lanjing Bridge was originally a bamboo cable suspension bridge and rebuilt into a beam bridge named Rainbow Bridge in 1295 during the Yuan Dynasty. The beam bridge was destroyed and rebuilt again into an iron cable suspension bridge between 1465 and 1487 during the Ming Dynasty. After many destructions and reconstructions, the extant suspension bridge was reconstructed in 1681. Emperor Kangxi personally inscribed "A Rainbow Flying to the Other Shore" for the bridge. An imperial library was built in the east side of the bridge to house his inscriptions.

The Rainbow Bridge stands magnificently over the deep, raging water of Lancang River with precipices on the west side and steep mountain peaks on the east side. It is 113.4m long and 3.7m wide with 18 iron cables, 16 load-bearing cables and 2 railing cables supported by 30 iron bars connecting

- 霁虹桥桥西崖壁上的题刻

由于此处景色壮美、古寺多，再加上古桥的雄伟，历代有许多著名文人来此游览，留下了许多诗文碑刻。在桥西的绝壁上，"霁虹桥""西南第一桥""人力所通""悬崖步渡"等摩崖石刻历历在目，多数字大盈尺，风骨高古，雄浑壮丽，颇有气魄。

Cliff Inscriptions to the West of the Rainbow Bridge

This place with beautiful scenery, ancient temples and the magnificent ancient bridge attracted many noted literati from different dynasties to visit here leaving behind many poetry inscriptions on the precipitous cliffs to the west of the Rainbow Bridge such as "Rainbow Bridge", "First Bridge in Southwest", "Road of Manpower", and "Walking Bridge over the Sheer Cliff". These gigantic cliff carvings are striking and majestic.

to both the railing and the load-bearing cables. On the bridge deck an iron clamp is installed every 6 meters to fasten the 16 load-bearing cables. Laid on top are planks tied by wires to the load-bearing cables. The cables are anchored firmly on the semicircular-shaped tower built on each end of the bridge, which also has a pavilion and a custom house, the one in the west long gone with the one in the east remaining.

> 双龙桥

双龙桥，坐落在云南建水城西的泸水与塌冲河会合处，所谓"双龙"，指塌冲河、泸江河，有一桥镇锁"双龙"之意。

双龙桥下共有17孔，桥全长153米，宽3米。此桥在清乾隆年间初建时只建了三孔桥洞。道光初年，这里暴雨成灾，山洪陡涨，河面增

- 双龙桥的桥面
  Double-Loong Bridge's Deck

> Double-Loong Bridge (Shuanglong Qiao)

The Double-Loong Bridge is situated at the intersection of Lujiang, River and Tachong River to the west of Jianshui City, Yunnan Province. "Double Loongs" refers to the Tachong River and the Lujiang River and the Double-Loong Bridge implies that one bridge could tame two loongs.

The Double-Loong Bridge has 17 arches, 153m long and 3m wide. The original bridge constructed during the reign of Emperor Qianlong of the Qing Dynasty only had three arches. In early 1821, torrential rains and flooding widened the river nearly 100 meters. The original three-arch bridge could no longer span the entire river. In 1839 fourteen more arches were connected to the original three arches with three pavilions built on top, a big one in the middle and two

• 云南建水双龙桥
Double-Loong Bridge of Jianshui County, Yunnan Province

宽了近百米，原先的三孔小桥无法再横贯两岸，因此在道光十九年（1839年）又增建石桥14孔，与原先的三孔桥首尾相连。桥上又建了三座阁楼，两端阁楼略小，居中一座雄伟壮观。此阁画栋雕梁，翘角飞檐，形态美观，阁下的基台宽度达到16.15米，凸出于桥体之外，因此楼阁和基台既是桥体的组成部分，又似乎是一座独立的建筑物。阁的底层是桥的通道，还设有楼梯，行人可以登阁远眺。这样的结构和造型，在中国现存的石拱桥中并不多见。桥南端还建有一座重檐八角的桥亭，高有十多米，玲珑秀丽，与桥中央的楼阁相互辉映。

smaller ones on the side. The middle pavilion has the most striking features with painted pillars, carved beams and upturned eaves. Standing on a 16.15m wide platform protruding from the bridge deck, the middle pavilion and the platform are a part of the bridge, but also look like an independent structure. The ground floor of the pavilion also serves as part of the bridge roadway with stairs for pedestrians to go up for an overlook. This kind of bridge structure and architectural style are hardly seen among extant ancient stone arch bridges in China. At the southern end of the bridge stands another 10m tall double-eave octagonal pavilion with refined and delicate design complementary to the pavilion in the center of the bridge.

> 梓里桥

梓里桥又名"金龙桥",位于云南丽江,横跨于金沙江上。清光绪二年(1876年),贵州官员蒋宗汉私人捐资修建该桥,工程历时5年,清光绪六年(1880年)此桥建成。桥的主体结构是16根粗大的铁

> Hometown Bridge (Zili Qiao)

The Hometown Bridge, also known as the "Golden Loong Bridge" (*Jinlong Qiao*), is situated in Lijiang City, Yunnan Province across the Jinsha River. The initial construction was funded by a private donation from Jiang Zonghan,

- 茶马古道上的梓里桥
  The Hometown Bridge on the Tea-Horse Ancient Route

链，两头悬系在两岸，其中14根为承重底链，上铺横竖两层木板，另两根铁链为两侧护栏。每根铁链均由约500个铁环相扣连接而成，桥总长116米，净跨90米，桥面宽3米。据说建桥时，运输建筑材料的骡子每次每匹只能驮运6只铁环，铁环全部被运到江边后，再用炉火加热、手工锻铸连接成大铁链。梓里桥是中国现存桥面最宽、铁链数量最多的铁索桥，同时也是金沙江上现存最古老的一座索桥。过去，这里是茶马古道上的重要通道，两岸各族群众和运送货物的马帮在桥上熙攘往来，十分热闹。

an official in Guizhou Province in 1876. It took five years to complete the bridge construction in 1880. The main structure consists of 16 iron cables suspended on either side of the riverbank. Fourteen of them are load-bearing cables, on which timber planks are placed horizontally and vertically in two layers. Two other cables are used as railings each comprising 500 iron links interlocked with each other. The bridge is 116m long and 3m wide with a 90m span. It is said that during the construction each mule could only carry 6 iron links at a time. When they were all brought to the riverside, the iron links were forged and built manually into large iron chains at the spot. The Hometown Bridge has the widest roadway and the largest number of iron links among the extant ancient iron cable suspension bridges in China. It is also the oldest suspension bridge existing on the Jinsha River today. As an important road in the Tea-Horse Ancient Route (*Chama Gudao*), the bridge witnessed a lot of bustling traffic of caravans and people of different ethnic groups from both sides of the bridge.

茶马古道

  茶马古道是存在于中国西南地区的民间贸易通道,源于唐宋时期的"茶马互市"。"茶马互市"是历史上汉藏民族间以茶易马或以马换茶的贸易往来,茶马贸易的兴盛不仅繁荣了古代西部地区的经济文化,也造就了茶马古道这条传播的路径。在这条古老而又神秘的道路之上,马帮源源不断地为藏族聚居区驮去茶叶、盐巴、布匹等生活必需品,再从藏族聚居区换回马匹、牛羊和皮毛,它是目前世界上已知的地势最高最险的文明传播古道。

Tea-Horse Ancient Route

The Tea-Horse Ancient Route originated from the "Tea and Horse Trading Market" in the Tang and Song dynasties where the Zang people and the Han people exchanged tea for horses or vice versa. It served as a transportation channel in the southwest of China. The rise of the tea-horse trade not only promoted economic and cultural prosperity of the western region, but also created the Tea-Horse Route. On this old and mysterious road, caravans continuously transported tea, salt, cloths and other necessities to the areas inhabited by the Zang people, and in turn brought back horses, cows, sheep and furs through exchanges with the Zang people. This is an ancient route to spread civilization in the highest and steepest location known in the world today.

- 茶马古道上的马帮
Caravans in the Tea-Horse Ancient Route

> 普修桥

　　普修桥坐落在湖南怀化市通道侗族自治县的坪坦河上。桥始建于清乾隆年间，后毁于洪水，清嘉庆八年（1803年）重修。桥全长57.7米，宽4.2米，是一座集桥、亭、廊于一体的木结构廊桥。全桥共有

• 普修桥
Puxiu Bridge

> Puxiu Bridge

The Puxiu Bridge crosses the Pingtan River in Tongdao Dong Autonomous County, Huaihua City, Hunan Province. Originally constructed during the reign of Emperor Qianlong of the Qing Dynasty, it was destroyed by flooding and rebuilt in 1803. It is a 57.7m long and 4.2m wide wooden structure that combines the styles of bridge, pavilion and corridor. A total of 21 corridor sections are decorated with

- 普修桥的桥亭
Pavilions on the Puxiu Bridge

21个廊间，桥廊两侧设置通长直棂窗，桥身的长廊分设三座桥亭，桥两端各设一座桥门。两边桥亭为三重檐，中间桥亭有七重密檐，下三层为方形平面，上四层为八角攒尖葫芦顶，顶尖有一只泥塑青鸟，能迎风转动，发出鸣响。桥亭檐角高挑，雕塑精致，曲线优美。

ancient-style wooden bar windows. The entire corridor is separated by three pavilions with two gateways standing at each end of the bridge. The side pavilions have triple eaves and the center pavilion has dense septuplet eaves with the lower triple eaves in a square shape and the upper quadruple eaves in a pointed octagonal shape. A clay sculpture of a black bird sits at the pointed top of the pavilion rotating and ringing in the wind. The bridge profile shows a beautiful curved line with the upturned eaves and the exquisite clay sculpture.

> 祝圣桥

祝圣桥位于贵州镇远,始建于明洪武二十一年(1388年),当初名为"舞溪桥",由镇远当地土司

> Zhusheng Bridge

The Zhusheng Bridge (meaning the bridge to celebrate the saint) in Zhenyuan County, Guizhou Province, was first constructed in 1388 during the Ming

• 镇远祝圣桥 (图片提供:FOTOE)
Zhusheng Bridge in Zhenyuan County

奏请朝廷修建。后因土司家族内部的纷争，以及朝廷推行"改土归流"的政策，修桥工程半途而废。万历三十七年（1609年），此桥得以重修，直至崇祯元年（1628年）才告竣工，前后历经约250年时间。桥建成后屡塌屡修，几百年间曾经过多次修复，其中一次修复竣工时，正值清康熙皇帝寿诞，于是桥被更名为"祝圣桥"。桥长135米，宽8.5米，高14米，在贵州乃至整个西南地区都是比较长的一座桥。这座桥全由青石建造，桥墩是明代的遗物，而桥身却是清代重建。祝圣桥中央建有一座楼阁，名叫魁星楼，为三层重檐八角攒尖顶结构，建于清光绪四年（1878年）。

Dynasty. Originally named Wuxi Bridge, it was proposed to the imperial court and built by the local chieftain of Zhenyuan. The construction was left unfinished due to some internal disputes among family members of the local chieftain and a policy change in the imperial court to reduce the power of local chieftains. The bridge was rebuilt in 1609 and completed by 1628 during the Ming Dynasty. Over the course of 250 years, it went through many collapses and reconstructions, one of which took place during the birthday celebration of the Emperor Kangxi. The bridge's name was then changed to "Zhusheng Bridge". It is 135m long, 8.5m wide and 14m high considered a relatively long bridge in Guizhou Province and even in the entire Southwest China. All built in bluestones, the bridge piers are relics of the Ming Dynasty and the body came from rebuilding in the Qing Dynasty. In the center of the bridge is the Kuixin Pavilion, a pointed triple-eave octagonal-shaped structure built in 1878.

> 洛阳桥

洛阳桥位于福建泉州东郊的洛阳江上，原名"万安桥"，是北宋时的泉州太守、著名书法家蔡襄（1012—1067）主持建造的。工程从皇祐五年（1053年）至嘉祐四年（1059年），前后历时6年，耗银14000两，才建成这座跨江接海

• 蔡襄像
Portrait of Cai Xiang

> Luoyang Bridge

The Luoyang Bridge, originally named Wan'an Bridge, crosses the Luoyang River in the east suburbs of Quanzhou, Fujian Province. Under the supervision of the famous calligrapher Cai Xiang (1012-1067), it took six years from 1053 to 1059 to finish this bridge that crossed a river and connected to the sea, at a cost of 14 thousand taels of silver. According to historical records, the bridge was extremely large in size with a length of 1,198.8m when it was first built. In the past 800 years after its completion, it was rebuilt 17 times. Currently it is 742.29m long, 4.5m wide and 7.3m high. The completion of this bridge not only connected both sides of the very wide Wan'an Crossing, but also opened up a land passageway from Guangdong and Fujian Provinces to the north of China, making the transportation of goods from

的大石桥。据记载，初建时桥长三百六十丈，规模巨大。此桥建成800余年来，先后经过17次大的修复。现桥长742.29米、宽4.5米、高7.3米。洛阳桥的建成不仅接通了"水阔五里"的万安渡，而且也连通了当时粤闽北上的陆路通道，使南来北往的货物畅通无阻。

洛阳桥在造桥技术上最大的成就在于成功地采用了"筏形基础"

the south to the north possible.

The greatest technical achievement of the Luoyang Bridge is to adopt the raft-style foundation and the method of accumulating stones at the bottom of the river. A huge quantity of stones was thrown into the river along the center line of the bridge to build a low dam at the bottom of the river. This is called raft foundation in modern bridge building

- 《万安桥记》碑拓片 蔡襄（北宋）

  据记载，北宋之前的洛阳江江流湍急，波涛汹涌，水深难测，常常造成翻船事故。因此当时泉州的地方官蔡襄就主持修建了洛阳桥。他还是宋代著名的书法家，曾经撰文并书写《万安桥记》碑，碑文短小精炼，行文流畅，书法优美，堪称古代碑刻精品。

  Stele Rubbing: *Chronicle of the Wan'an Bridge*, Northern Song Dynasty (960-1127)

  It is documented that boats were often overturned in the deep raging Luoyang River before the Northern Song Dynasty. Therefore Cai Xiang, a local official decided to supervise the construction of the Luoyang Bridge. He was also a famous calligrapher in the Northern Song Dynasty and wrote the *Chronicle of the Wan'an Bridge* as the inscription for the stele. The writing is short and simple with elegant calligraphy. It is considered one of the best stele inscriptions in ancient China.

和"种蛎固基法"。人们沿着桥梁的中线向水中抛置大量石块，形成一条横跨江底的矮石堤，然后在上面建造桥墩，这在现代桥梁技术中被称为"筏型基础"。为了抵挡湍急的水流，建造者又在桥墩下的浅海中大量养殖牡蛎，利用这种软体动物附着力强和繁殖迅速的特性，将桥基和桥墩石胶结成牢固的整体，使之经得起水流的冲撞。

technology. In order to resist rapid water flow, large quantities of oysters were cultivated below the bridge piers in order to take the advantage of mollusk characteristics of strong attachment and rapid reproduction, which firmly glued the bridge piles and piers together as one structure so that they could withstand strong currents.

The Luoyang Bridge has over 300 stone beams, each weighing 7 to 8 tons.

● 福建泉州洛阳桥（图片提供：FOTOE）
Luoyang Bridge of Quanzhou City, Fujian Province

洛阳桥的石梁共有300余块，每条石梁都有七八吨重。在古代没有现代吊装设备的情况下，要在水面上架设如此巨大的石梁是一大难事。为此，人们采取了"浮运架梁法"，即将开采好的石梁事先放在木浮排上，等到两个临近的桥墩完成后，就趁涨潮时将木排划入两个桥墩之间，等到潮水一退，木排下降，石梁就落到石墩上了。

In the past it was a big problem to erect huge stone beams over the water without any lifting equipment. Therefore, people first put a big stone beam on a wood raft. When the construction of two piers was completed, they would wait until high tide to move the raft between them. When the tide retreated, the raft subsequently lowered with the water and the stone beam was automatically placed on top of the two piers.

> 安平桥

安平桥横跨在福建晋江安海镇和南安水头镇之间的海湾上，因安海镇古称安平道，因此得名"安平桥"。安平桥属于古代连梁式的

> Anping Bridge

The Anping Bridge stands across the bay between Shuitou Town of Nan'an City and Anhai Town of Jinjiang City in Fujian Province. Anhai Town was called Anping Road in the past, hence the name Anping Bridge. It was built as a connected-beam stone slab bridge. The construction started in 1138 during the Southern Song Dynasty and took 14 years to complete. Originally the bridge was 2,255m long, about 5 Chinese miles;

- 晋江安海镇的安平桥（图片提供：FOTOE）
安平桥是中国现存最长的古代石桥，享有"天下无桥长此桥"之誉。
Anping Bridge of Anhai Town, Jinjiang City
The Anping Bridge is the oldest ancient stone bridge existing in China today. It has the fame of "no bridge in the world longer than this bridge".

石板平桥，始建于南宋绍兴八年（1138年），历时14年建成。桥全长原为2255米，约合五华里，所以又俗称"五里桥"，现长2070米。桥面宽3米—3.8米，桥下共有361个桥墩，用花岗岩条石交错叠砌而成。

桥上筑有5座供行人休息的"憩亭"，东端为水心亭，西端为海潮庵，中部的中亭规模最大，面宽10米，周围有历代修桥留下的碑记16方，亭前还伫立着两尊护桥将军像；在三亭中间还有两座雨亭。桥面两侧有石护栏，栏柱头雕刻狮子、蟾蜍等形象。桥两侧的水中筑有4座对称的方形石塔，还有一座圆塔。桥的入口处有一座五层白塔，高22米，为平面六角形的空心砖塔。

therefore it was also known as "the Five-mile Bridge". Currently the bridge is 2,070m long with a deck width between 3m and 3.8m. There are 361 piers built with layers of granite stone slabs.

The bridge has five "Rest Pavilion" for pedestrians. The Water Center Pavilion (*Shuixin Ting*) stands at the east end of the bridge and the Sea Tide Pavilion (*Haichao An*) at the west end of the bridge. The pavilion in the middle is the largest with a 10m width, around which there are 16 stele inscriptions left from reconstructions of the bridge in different dynasties. In front of the center pavilion stand statues of two warriors guarding the bridge. In between the three pavilions there are two pavilions serving as rain shelters. Lions and toads were carved at the top of the posts supporting the stone railings. In the water on each side of the bridge sit four symmetrical square-shape stone pagodas and a round pagoda. At the bridgehead there is a five-story 22m high white tower with a hexagonal plane and built in hollow bricks.

> 江东桥

江东桥原名"虎渡桥",是一座多孔梁式石桥,位于福建九龙江北溪下游。这里地处九龙江北溪与西溪交汇入海处,两岸峻山夹峙,

> Jiangdong Bridge

The Jiangdong Bridge, originally called the Hudu Bridge, is a stone beam bridge of multiple openings, which is situated at the north downstream of the Jiulong River, Fujian Province. It is at

• 福建漳州江东桥（图片提供: FOTOE）
Jiangdong Bridge of Zhangzhou City, Fujian Province

江宽流急，地势险要，古称"三省通衢"。宋绍熙元年（1190年），这里曾架过木浮桥，嘉定七年（1214年）始建石墩木桥，嘉熙元年（1237年）木桥被大火烧毁，于是建成梁式石桥。1970年，古桥上加建钢筋混凝土公路桥。如今在靠西岸公路桥下，尚存古桥的五座完整桥墩、两跨桥面及残墩基9座。

江东桥的石梁每条长22米—23米、宽1.15米—1.5米、厚1.3米—1.6米、重近200吨。在古代要开采如此巨大石梁，其难度是不可设想的，而用什么工具将其运到江边，架上桥墩，至今还是一个谜。

the intersection between the north stream and the west stream of the Jiulong River before they flow into the sea. Situated in a tough terrain of a narrow strait between two steep mountains with a rapid water flowing below, this place was known as the "thoroughfare for three provinces" in the past. In 1190 during the Song Dynasty a floating bridge of timber was once built here. In 1214 a timber beam bridge of stone piers was constructed, but burned down in a big fire in 1237. Then the bridge was rebuilt into a stone beam bridge. In 1970 a reinforced concrete highway bridge was added on top of the ancient bridge. Today in the west side under the highway bridge there are still some remaining parts of the ancient bridge including five bridge piers in very good condition, two sections of the bridge deck and remnants of nine bridge piles.

Each of the stone beams of the Jiandong Bridge is 22-23m long, 1.15-1.5m wide and 1.3-1.6m thick weighing about 200 tons. It is hard to imagine and it is still a mystery how these big stone beams were mined, what transportation vehicles were used to ship them to the riverbank and how they were placed on the bridge piles.

> 东关桥

东关桥位于福建永春县东关镇东美村的湖洋溪上，是福建最早的木梁廊桥之一，也是闽南地区鲜见的长廊屋盖梁式古桥。东关桥始建于南宋绍兴十五年（1145年），又名"通仙桥"。据载，南宋年间的东关桥是敞天桥，后来为防止雨水的侵蚀并供行人歇脚，明弘治十三年（1500年），当地人在桥上建造了20间木屋，形成廊桥。现存的东关桥为清光绪元年（1875年）复建。桥全长85米，宽5米，桥下有4个船形的桥墩，都用青石筑成。墩下以大松木作卧桩，承载整座桥梁；墩上用巨石叠成三层支架大梁。每个桥孔都由22根长16米—18米的特大杉木作梁铺设成上、下两层。桥上以砖石砌墙，用木料作柱

> Dongguan Bridge

The Dongguan Bridge is situated on the Huyang Creek of Dongmei Village in Dongguan Town, Yongchun County, Fujian Province. It is one of the oldest corridor bridges of timber in Fujian Province with a regular roof-style cover over the long corridor, a style rarely seen in south Fujian Province. The bridge was originally constructed in 1145 during the Southern Song Dynasty and named "To Immortal Bridge" (*Tongxian Qiao*). According to historical documentations, the bridge in the Southern Song Dynasty was an open bridge and in 1500 during the Ming Dynasty 20 wooden covered sections were built on the bridge deck to form a long corridor to protect the bridge from rain erosion and as rest places for pedestrians. The extant bridge is rebuilt in 1875 during the Qing Dynasty, 85m long and 5m wide with four boat-shape piers

檩、桥板、护栏。虽然几经复建和大修，但今天的东关桥依然较完整地保留着宋代桥梁的建筑特点。

made of bluestones. Large pine wood were placed under the piers to bear the weight of the entire bridge. Three levels of big rocks were laid on top of the piers to support the big timber beams. Twenty-two beams made of 16-18m long huge Chinese fir were installed in two layers for each bridge opening. The bridge deck has brick walls, wooden railings, panels and posts. Even though it went through several reconstructions and big repairs, the current Dongguan Bridge still maintains the characteristics of the the bridge style of the Song Dynasty.

- 福建永春东关桥（图片提供：CFP）
  Dongguan Bridge of Yongchun County, Fujian Province

> 湘子桥

湘子桥位于广东省潮州市的东门外，横跨于韩江之上。此桥初名"济川桥"，后名"广济桥"，俗称"湘子桥"，这是中国最早的一座开关活动式的大石桥。

据史料记载，湘子桥初建于南宋时期。全桥的总长度为517.3米，桥面的宽度为5米。由于桥的规模很大，修建的时间也较长。桥分为三段，桥的东段长283米，有桥墩13座，从南宋绍熙元年（1190年）动工，至开禧二年（1206年）完成，历时16年；西段长137米，有桥墩10座，从南宋乾道六年（1170年）开工建设，到宝庆二年（1226年）完成，历时56年；中段长97.3米，是用24只木船搭成的浮桥，连接着东段和西段。

> Xiangzi Bridge

The Xiangzi Bridge lies across the Hanjiang River outside of the east gate of Chaozhou City, Guangdong Province. It was originally named Jichuan Bridge, and later Guangji Bridge. Commonly known as Xiangzi Bridge, it is the earliest stone bridge in China that can move to open and close.

According to historical records, the original bridge, constructed in the Southern Song Dynasty, was 517.3m long and 5m wide at the bridge deck. Because of its large scale the construction took a long time. The bridge was divided into three sections. It took 16 years from 1190 to 1206 to complete the east section of 13 piers with a length of 283m and another 56 years from 1170 to 1226 to complete the west section of 10 piers with a length of 137m. The middle section was a 97.3m long floating bridge

济川桥自修建之日起，由于洪水、台风、地震和战火等的破坏，曾多次毁建，据记载，史上经过大修或重建至少有24次。明弘治年间重修时，还在桥墩上建亭20座，此后又在桥墩上修建了24座形式不同的楼阁。清雍正年间，在浮桥的左右桥墩上各置铁牛一只，铁牛背上铸有"镇桥御水"四个字。道光二十二年(1842年)大水冲毁东岸桥墩，一只铁牛跌入河中，不久后在河中发现。另一只在1939年遭日本飞机轰炸，不知去向。

of 24 boats connecting the east and the west sections.

It is documented that the bridge went through at least 24 major repairs and reconstructions after its completion due to damages caused by floods, typhoons, earthquakes and wars. Between 1488 and 1505 in the Ming Dynasty, 20 pavilions were built on the piers during its reconstruction. Afterwards 24 pavilions of different styles were added. During the reign of Emperor Yongzheng of the Qing Dynasty, a cow sculpture cast in iron was placed on the pier at each end of the floating bridge. On the back of the cow

- 湘子桥俯瞰（图片提供：全景正片）
  An Overlook of the Xiangzi Bridge

湘子桥的桥墩十分宽大，其宽度为5.7米—10.8米，长度为14.4米—21.7米，如此巨大的桥墩在中国古代桥梁中是不多见的。因为韩江河宽浪急，河中立墩困难；东西两段的桥墩过分宽大，不利于河水的通过。浮桥的设置不仅扩大了桥下的过水面积，克服桥墩宽大带来的困难，又有利于大型海船和木排在桥下通过。

- 湘子桥中段的十八梭船浮桥（图片提供：FOTOE）
Eighteen-boat Floating Fridge in the Middle Section of the Xiangzi Bridge

carved four Chinese characters *Zhen Qiao Yu Shui* meaning "an important bridge over the imperial water". In 1842, floods destroyed the east part of the bridge and one cow fell into the water, which was discovered later in the river. The other cow disappeared in the bombing by the Japanese invaders in 1939.

The piers of the Xiangzi Bridge have a width from 5.7m to 10.8m and a length from 14.4m to 21.7m each. Piers of this huge size are very rare in the Chinese ancient bridges. The immensely wide and raging Hanjiang River made it very difficult to build piers in the center of the river. In addition the piers on the east and west sections of the bridge are so huge that there is no enough space for water to go through. Therefore, the installation of a floating bridge in the center not only resolved the problem caused by the huge piers, but also increased the space for water to flow through, thereby allowing enough clearance for big ships and rafts to sail through.

> 程阳桥

程阳桥，又叫"永济桥""盘龙桥"，坐落在广西三江的林溪河上。这是一座木石结构的大桥，桥长64.4米，宽3.4米，高10.6米。在五个石砌的桥墩上铺设木板，桥上建有遮雨的长廊，两旁有长凳，可供行人避雨和休息。五个桥墩上又建有侗族风格的桥亭五座，屋面均为四层重檐塔式建筑，飞檐高翘，神采飞扬。廊檐绘有精美的侗族图案，整个桥面的廊楼建筑造型美观，风格别致。

程阳桥整座桥梁用大木凿榫接合，不用一钉一铆，大小木条纵横交错，一丝不差，结构精密，令人惊叹。

> Chengyang Bridge

The Chengyang Bridge, also known as Yongji Bridge and Panlong Bridge, sits across the Linxi River in Sanjiang Dong Autonomous County, Guangxi Zhuang Autonomous Region. It is a large bridge with a structure of timber and stone with a 64.4m length, 3.4m width and 10.6m height. Timber planks are laid on top of the five stone piers. A long covered corridor is built on the deck with long benches on both sides for pedestrians to rest and use as shelters from the rain. Additionally on the bridge there are five beautiful four-story double-eave pavilions of the Dong ethnic style with exquisitely carved beams of Dong ethnic patterns.

The entire Chengyang Bridge did not use a single nail or rivet, but was dovetailed by interlocking tenons and mortises. The structural precision of crisscrossed wood blocks is truly

● **广西三江程阳桥** (图片提供：FOTOE)

奇特精巧的风雨桥，高大雄伟的鼓楼，别具风格的民居，映着青山绿水，组成了一幅秀丽的风俗画卷。

Chengyang Bridge of Sanjiang Dong Autonomous County, Guangxi Zhuang Autonomous Region

This unique and exquisite corridor bridge unfolds an enchanting scroll painting of folk culture with magnificent pavilions and houses in a distinctive style against a background of green mountains and clear water.

> 仙桂桥

　　仙桂桥位于广西阳朔白沙乡的遇龙河支流上，是广西最古老的单孔石拱桥。此桥为南北走向，初建于北宋宣和五年（1123年），南宋绍兴七年（1137年）重修。桥长约26米，宽4.2米，高2.2米，拱跨6.9米，桥面铺石板，两端各有踏跺四级。

　　仙桂桥桥体结构的奇特之处在于，桥拱采取了极为罕见的并列砖法，用9组券石拱砌，共用石281块并列而成。历经八百多年风雨剥蚀和洪流冲击，桥体仍完好无损。桥下拱券上刻有记录此桥初建及重修过程的文字，有了这些模糊的字迹，人们才得以了解仙桂桥的历史。

> Xiangui Bridge

The Xiangui Bridge is the oldest single-arch stone bridge in Guangxi across a tributary of the Yulong River from south to north at Baisha Village, Yangshuo County, Guangxi Zhuang Autonomous Region. It was initially constructed in 1123 during the Northern Song Dynasty and rebuilt in 1137 during the Southern Song Dynasty. It is almost 26m long, 4.2m wide and 2.2m high with a 6.9m span. The bridge deck is paved with stone slabs, four levels of steps at each side.

　　What is extraordinary about the Xiangui Bridge lies in the construction of the arch with 9 pairs of bricks laid in paralleled fashion from both sides up to the center using a total of 281 stone bricks. This bridge building method is very rare among ancient bridges in China. The bridge is in perfect condition even after over eight hundred years of rain erosion and flooding. On the side of arch carved the documentation of the bridge's initial construction and the rebuilding from which visitors can learn about the history of the bridge.

• 广西阳朔仙桂桥（图片提供：FOTOE）
Xiangui Bridge of Yangshuo County, Guangxi Zhuang Autonomous Region

> 花桥

花桥位于广西桂林的东门外，横跨在漓江支流小东江和灵剑江交汇处的水面上。桥东有一块高达十余米的巨石，人称"芙蓉石"，又称"天柱石"，因此花桥又称为"天柱桥"。

花桥始建于宋代，初名"嘉熙桥"，原是一座五孔石桥。元代，这座石桥被洪水冲毁，明景泰七年（1456年）得以重修，并改为木梁桥；嘉靖十九年（1540年）再度重建，并改建为石拱桥，更名为"花桥"。1965年重建时，桥上的木构件改为钢筋混凝土构件，现在的花桥长125.2米，桥面宽6.3米，桥高7.2米。花桥是一座薄墩联拱石桥，分为两段，一段为旱桥，一段为水桥。旱桥有七孔，桥孔的跨度从东

> Flower Bridge *(Hua Qiao)*

The Flower Bridge is situated outside of the east gate of Guilin city, Guangxi Zhuang Autonomous Region across the junction between the Xiaodong River, a small stream of Lijiang River and Lingjian River. To the east of the bridge stands a huge rock of over ten meters high. People call it "Lotus Flower Rock" or "Heavenly Pillar Rock" (*Tianzhu Shi*). Therefore the Flower Bridge is also known as the Heavenly Pillar Bridge.

It was a five-arch stone bridge initially constructed in the Song Dynasty and originally named Jiaxi Bridge. Destroyed by flooding in the Yuan Dynasty, it was rebuilt in 1456 during the Ming Dynasty into a timber beam bridge. In 1540 it was reconstructed again into a stone arch bridge and named the Flower Bridge. The reconstruction of 1965 replaced some of the wooden parts with reinforced concrete

往西逐渐减小。旱桥起着引桥的作用，减缓了桥面的坡度，洪水季节还可排水，设计十分精妙。水桥有四孔，各孔跨度较大，加上拱墩很薄，使桥孔几乎相连。桥亭的屋面一律铺成绿色琉璃瓦，风平浪静的时候，半圆形的拱券倒映水中，就像是四轮圆月，景色动人。

- 桂林花桥
  Flower Bridge in Guilin City

components. The current Flower Bridge is 125.2m long, 6.3m wide and 7.2m high with continuous spans and slender piers. The bridge is divided into two sections: a section over the water and a section on land. There are seven arches on the land section with each span gradually becoming smaller from east to west. This section functions as a bridge approach to reduce the slope of the bridge deck and is also smartly designed to drain excessive water during flooding. The section over water has four arches with a relatively big span. The arches are almost next to each other due to their large span and the thin-walled piers. The roof of the pavilion on top of the bridge deck is made of glazed green tiles. It is a very enchanting sight when the semicircular arches are reflected on the water as if there were four full moons in the calm river.